THE
YANKEE
QUIZBOOK

THE YANKEE QUIZBOOK

Bob Weil

and

Jim Fitzgerald

Introduction by

Roger Kahn

Photo Research by
Robert Rodriguez

Dolphin Books
Doubleday & Company, Inc.
Garden City, New York
1981

Copyright © 1981 by Robert Weil and James W. Fitzgerald Jr.

Library of Congress Cataloging in Publication Data
Weil, Robert, 1955–
    The Yankee quiz book.

    (A Dolphin book)
    1. New York (City). Baseball Club (American League)
—Miscellanea. I. Fitzgerald, James William, Jr., 1948–
joint author. II. Title.
GV875.N4W44   796.357'64'097471   80-1654
ISBN 0-385-17178-1

Book design by James W. Fitzgerald Jr.

Dolphin Books

Doubleday & Company Inc.

All Rights Reserved

Printed in the United States of America

First Printing

ACKNOWLEDGMENTS

Baseball has always been a game demanding the combined talents of a whole host of people. Early on we discovered that *The Yankee Quiz Book* would be no different.

No greater tribute can be extended than to the New York Yankees, a team which has nurtured the devotion of generations of New Yorkers. Our irreverence is directed playfully, out of a spirit of respect rather than derision. The Yankees were extremely cooperative, if not slightly mystified, in answering our questions in Fort Lauderdale. Players, the likes of Mickey Mantle, Reggie Jackson and Tommy John, gave unsparingly of their time, as did Larry Wahl, Mickey Morabito and Joe D'Ambrosio in the media relations office. George Steinbrenner matched wits with us in the dugout, a sportsman all the way.

Outside of the Yankee organization, others contributed generously of their expertise and time, especially Nancy Boyland, the Eliasbergs, Holly Fitzgerald, Talbot Katz, Pam Lyons, Bob Morgan, John Redding, head librarian at the Cooperstown Hall of Fame, John Samson for his construction of the crossword puzzles, Stephanie Vardavas, Joan Walton and Margery Weinblatt. Writers Maury Allen, whose fondness for The 'Ol Professor was inspiring, Ed Linn and Lou Sahadi acted as veteran baseball sages in providing advice.

The following books proved especially useful: *The Baseball Encyclopedia* from MacMillan; *The Bronx Zoo* by Sparky Lyle and Peter Golenbock; *Catfish: The Three Million Dollar Pitcher* by Bill Libby; *Catching* by Elston Howard; *The Comeback* by Ryne Duren with Robert Drury; *Damn Yankee: The Billy Martin Story* by Maury Allen; *Dynasty: The New York Yankees 1949-1964* by Peter Golenbock; *New York Yankees 1980 Media Guide*; *Roger Maris at Bat* by Roger Maris and Jim Ogle; *This Date in New York Yankee History* by Nathan Salant (a mandatory Bible for any Yankeephile); *The Tommy John Story* by Tommy John and Sally John with Joe Messer; *The Ultimate Baseball Book* by Dan Okrent; *Whitey and Mickey: An Autobiography of the Yankee Years* by Whitey Ford, Mickey Mantle and Joe Durso; and *You Could Look It Up: The Life of Casey Stengel* by Maury Allen.

Photographs appearing on pages: 14, 21 (bottom), 23, 31 (bottom left), 36, 40, 43, 54, 73, 99 (center and bottom right), 100, 104, 105 (upper left), 109, and 113 are courtesy of U.P.I. Photograph appearing at the top of page 39 is courtesy of The Samuel Goldwyn Company. Photographs appearing on pages: 27, 91 (top and bottom), 102 and 127 are courtesy of A.P. All other photographs are courtesy of the Yankee archives.

Special thanks must be given to our editor Barry Lippman, and his associate Paul Aron, who gave encouragement from the start, to Rod Rodriguez, whose eye for collecting photographs matched the tone of the book, to Roger Kahn, as astute and elegant an observer of the game as anyone today, to our agent Wendy Lipkind who believed in the project even before it was created, and to the hundreds of Yankee players and millions of baseball fans who've made the Yankees the legendary team they are today.

Bob Weil and Jim Fitzgerald
New York, New York

CONTENTS

INTRODUCTION

When I was growing up in Brooklyn, I thought of the New York Yankees as a collective pin-striped eminence, always grinding down the Dodgers in October. Later I encountered Casey Stengel, an implausibly amusing character, but there was a certain calculation to the Stengel japery. When ol' Charlie Dressen dislocated syntax, he simply didn't know any better. Stengel's word-play, like Hamlet's to Polonius, was calculated. (I mean, Casey could have spoke as good as I or you.)

Finally I spent time with the Steinbrenner Yankees, when the press was firing Billy Martin and Martin was firing Reggie Jackson. Fun? Ask Al Rosen how much fun that was. (And pass the Valium.) In the unrelenting grip of my Brooklyn background, the Yankees seemed either inhuman, or too damn human to enjoy.

Now come Bob Weil and Jim Fitzgerald, certified, card-carrying Yankee fans, with a delightfully irreverent collection of questions and answers.

Which of Jackson's twenty-seven cars is his personal favorite? Why did neighborhood boys make fun of the young Billy Martin? Which Yankee lists his hobby as reading? Who pitched the most seasons as a Yankee? When did Babe Ruth win his only Most Valuable Player Award? Which Yankee hero's all-time most quotable quote is a commercial plug for a bank? This is talking baseball in high style. By any definition, no matter where you're from, wherever your heart may lie during the baseball season, this is indeed great fun.

There is a need and timeliness to baseball fun in 1981. Newspapers are crowded with stories of labor negotiations, contract terms and legal boilerplate. The network sportscasters are so chronically cheerful that they become depressing. The natural joyousness of the game is drowned.

You can, as Woody Allen suggests seriously, see baseball as an American art form. On another level you can look at it as a metaphor for time. The typical ball player, even the typical Yankee, goes from obscurity to fame and back in a decade. But unless you are actually involved as a player, a manager, or a club-owner, you had better recognize baseball as a grand entertainment.

Part unfolds on what Red Smith has called the green and brown and white geometry of the field. But part of the entertainment springs from the minor art of talking the game.

Who'dya rather have in center, Mantle or Snider or Mays?

Say, if Ted Williams played in the Stadium, he'd hit sixty home runs every year.

Yeah, and if DiMag played up in Fenway, he'd hit seventy.

Listen. Did you hear what Stengel did to those Congressmen who were trying to investigate baseball? He out-talked twenty-three politicians in one day.

Here then is an unpretentious and loving Yankee book that provides enough fact, nostalgia, trivia and fun to fuel weeks of splendid baseball talk. I think Messrs. Weil and Fitzgerald are on to something, perhaps the first work in a series. I hope their loyalties allow them to carry on their researches in Brooklyn and Los Angeles.

Long ago a Dodger rookie appeared whose name was Fladgett Zunk. Mr. Zunk did not make the club, but subsequently sportswriters ran an annual Fladgett Zunk Odd Name Sweepstakes.

Question: Who won the Zunk competition in 1955?

Answer: Odbert Herman Hamric.

Mr. Hamric came to bat once, made out, and did not again wear a Dodger uniform.

All right, gentlemen. To your sequel.

—Roger Kahn

THE
YANKEE
QUIZBOOK

BUCKY

1. Any Yankee fan can remember Bucky's three-run homer against Boston in the 1978 playoff game, but who was the Bosox hurler who surrendered the fatal hit?
    - a. Luis Tiant   b. Dennis Eckersley   c. Mike Torrez
    - d. Bill Lee

2. Lady fans will be disappointed to learn that Bucky got married at the age of _____ (18, 19, 21, 23) in 1970.

3. Dent was traded to the Yankees at the beginning of the 1977 season from which team?
    - a. Chicago White Sox   b. Pittsburgh Pirates
    - c. Oakland Athletics   d. Detroit Tigers

4. Which of the following cars would you be likely to find Bucky Dent driving?
    - a. 1942 Rolls Royce   b. Cadillac Seville   c. '68 Ford Mustang
    - d. '57 Ford Thunderbird   e. BMW   f. Diesel Mercedes

5. Despite being named MVP in the 1978 World Series, Dent's World Series batting average of .417 was second to the .438 average of
    - a. Graig Nettles   b. Reggie Jackson   c. Mickey Rivers
    - d. Brian Doyle

6. Which former American League pitcher does Dent feel gives him the most trouble?
    - a. Mike Caldwell   b. Jim Palmer   c. Mike Flanagan
    - d. Nolan Ryan

7. In the tradition of many Yankee shortstops, Dent has been a premier fielder but has never distinguished himself at the plate. As a Yankee batter (1977–1979) what has been Dent's highest batting average?
    - a. .230   b. .243   c. .247   d. .254

8. Which one of the following products has Dent *not* endorsed?
    - a. fur coats   b. Easter Seals   c. Murjani jeans
    - d. picture posters

9. Name Dent's favorite ballpark to hit in.

JOLTIN' JOE DIMAGGIO

1. As a young player, Joe DiMaggio did not know what a quote was when a reporter asked him for one. He thought it was a
   a. soft drink   b. autograph   c. photograph   d. telephone number

2. DiMaggio struck out _____ (13, 29, 32, 86) times in the 1941 season, the year he hit in fifty-six consecutive games.

3. After the end of Joe's remarkable 1941 season, General Manager Ed Barrow
   a. gave Joe a bonus of $10,000 for his performance.
   b. tried to cut Joe's salary by $2,500 and called him greedy.
   c. attempted to prevent Uncle Sam from drafting DiMaggio.
   d. raised Joe's salary to $85,000, a record sum at that time.

4. DiMaggio played for only thirteen seasons with the Yankees. In how many of those years did he compete in a World Series?
   a. 7   b. 9   c. 10   d. 11

5. DiMaggio's father, a San Francisco resident, did what for a living?
   a. drove a streetcar up and down Nob Hill
   b. managed a restaurant on Fisherman's Wharf
   c. was a crab fisherman
   d. was the maitre d' at the Fairmont Hotel

6. "Joltin' Joe DiMaggio" was a hit song of the 1940s. Who sang it?
   a. Alan Courtney   b. Frank Sinatra   c. Perry Como
   d. Rosemary Clooney

7. As an aging veteran during the 1950 and 1951 seasons, Joe acted as a friend and protege for the young
   a. Mickey Mantle   b. Billy Martin   c. Phil Rizzuto
   d. Whitey Ford

8. True or false. Joe DiMaggio's .357 batting average led the League in 1941.

9. A half dozen roses are placed on the grave of Marilyn Monroe, reportedly by Joe DiMaggio, how often?
   a. once a month   b. once a week   c. twice a week
   d. three times a week

MARIS' ASSAULT ON THE BABE

1. What do Pedro Ramos, Gary Bell, Bill Monbouquette, Joe Nuxhall, Juan Pizarro, Hank Aguirre and Milt Pappas have in common?

2. Name this speaker if you can. "I have the highest regard for Roger Maris. He's a fine hitter. But I must admit I'm glad he didn't equal the Babe's sixty (in 154 games)."
   a. Johnny "Big Cat" Mize   b. Mrs. Claire Ruth   c. Casey Stengel
   d. Mickey Mantle

3. Everyone knows that Tracy Stallard yielded Maris' sixty-first home run, but who was the victim of his 60th?
   a. Hoyt Wilhelm   b. Frank Lary   c. Herb Score
   d. Jack Fisher

True or False.

_____ 4. Even though Maris hit sixty-one home runs in 1961, he lost the MVP award to Mickey Mantle.

_____ 5. Only once during the '61 season did Maris slug three home runs in a game.

_____ 6. Maris hit more of his sixty-one homers during night games than day games.

_____ 7. One result of the pressure of the 1961 season was that much of Maris' hair fell out.

_____ 8. Eddie Gaedel was the lucky eighteen-year-old lad who caught Maris' sixty-first home run in the Yankee bleachers.

9. *Trivia stumper.* What do radical folksinger Bob Dylan and Roger Maris have in common?

FAVORITE YANKEE OF ALL-TIME

Every Yankee fan has his or her favorite player, whether he be Ruth, Mantle or Virgil Trucks. Can you guess the all-time Yankee favorites of the players themselves? Fill in the blanks.

Bobby Murcer, raised in Oklahoma, a Sooner patriot all the way, picked ____1____ as his favorite Yankee of all time. Whitey Ford agreed with Murcer and also chose ____2____ as the Yankee whom he most admired. In fact, ____3____ (33%, 43%, 52%, 60%) of all the Yankees polled chose the immortal Number 7 player.

Whitey Ford garnered the most votes of all Yankee hurlers. It was no surprise that ____4____, the left-handed ace from Louisiana whose current winning percentage record rivals Ford, picked Whitey. It may also be predictable that Yogi Berra and Rick Cerone remained loyal to their Italian ancestry and named ____5____ as their favorite player. But then ____6____, a slugger from Oakland who might easily have named ____7____ as his best-loved Yankee, also selected the Yankee Clipper as Number 1 on his list. Only ____8____, a Yankee outfielder who drives a Rolls Royce and owns a discotheque, chose himself. ____9____, forever the measured and cautious diplomat, said that it would be "too tough" to name a favorite Yankee player, but rest assured he did not think of his favorite ex-manager, ____10____.

Jim Spencer, the steady, well-respected first baseman, was the only player to choose ____11____, an immortal first baseman also remembered for his dependability. Willie Randolph, a quiet and talented infielder, named ____12____, a quiet and talented outfielder who has departed for Japan. And Paul Blair selected ____13____, the catcher who must have thrown him out many times when he was trying to steal bases for Baltimore.

Fame, we learned, fades quickly. ____14____, the most feared and revered slugger of the century, was picked by not a single player.

(Left) Not everybody's favorite Yankee is Mickey Mantle or Joe DiMaggio. Some of the favorites are those who played steady everyday baseball. Identify each of the following favorites in this Yankee gallery.

TRADES AND PLAYS OF MIKE KEKICH AND FRITZ PETERSON

Baseball is a game of swapping and trading. You begin with baseball cards as a kid, you buy your first used car as a teen, who knows what comes as an adult? Fill in the blanks.

1. The Yanks sent outfielder Andy Kosco to the Dodgers in 1968 and acquired _____.

2. The Yankees acquired first baseman _____ and pitcher _____ as well as Cecil Upshaw in the trade that sent Fritz Peterson to Cleveland in 1974.

3. Following a tumultuous spring remembered more for its off than on the field plays, Mike Kekich was dealt in 1973 to the _____ (Chicago White Sox, Cleveland Indians, Seattle Mariners) for fireballer Lowell Palmer.

4. Kekich played a stint with the Nippon Ham Fighters in the country of _____ after being released in 1973.

5. Before retiring from the game, Fritz Peterson pitched for the _____ (Texas Rangers, Detroit Tigers, Cleveland Indians) after he had been traded to them for pitcher Stan Perzanowski.

6. Both Kekich and Peterson left the _____ organization bound for _____. Their professional trading was overshadowed however by their _____ swap in which _____ teamed up and married _____ while _____ briefly hooked up with _____ but then went his separate way.

WHAT A NUMBER!

Match the Yankee with his retired number.

1.	Lou Gehrig	**A.**	#5
2.	Whitey Ford	**B.**	#8
3.	Casey Stengel	**C.**	#7
4.	Bill Dickey	**D.**	#15
5.	Babe Ruth	**E.**	#37
6.	Joe DiMaggio	**F.**	#8
7.	Yogi Berra	**G.**	#16
8.	Thurman Munson	**H.**	#3
9.	Mickey Mantle	**I.**	#4

Name this fleet-footed shortstop from Boston pictured with the Bambino.

1. Baseball is a game of headaches, but first baseman Wally Pipp's headache on June 1, 1925, is more famous than most. What was the occasion?

2. This Hall-of-Fame outfielder, nicknamed "The Kentucky Colonel," stroked out 231 hits in the 1927 season, still a Yankee record. Name him.
   a. Bob Meusel   b. Earle Combs   c. Babe Ruth   d. Joe Dugan

3. The following four events all occurred in the 1920s. Can you put them in their correct chronological order?
   a. The Yankees clinch their first American League pennant against the Philadelphia Athletics.
   b. Babe Ruth is purchased from Boston for $125,000.
   c. The Yankees win the pennant by nineteen games and sport a 110–44 record, their highest winning percentage ever.
   d. Yankee Stadium is opened, and the Yankees defeat Boston, 4–1.

4. Numbers were added to Yankee players' uniforms in 1929. What logical method was used to give the players the appropriate number?

THE 1920S

One of the most famous Yankee infielders of the "Roaring 20s," he led the League in 1926 with ninety-six strikeouts. Who is he?

5. The feuds of Reggie Jackson and Billy Martin reminded old-timers of the rancor which existed between Babe Ruth and manager Miller Huggins in the 1920s. What prank did Ruth enjoy pulling most on the little Yankee manager?
   a. He would send strange women up to Huggins' hotel room.
   b. He would hold Huggins out of the windows of moving trains.
   c. He would play his harmonica on the team bus after the Yankees lost.
   d. He would wear his uniform purposely backwards to infuriate Huggins.

6. His brother Irish played for the New York Giants and Brooklyn Dodgers, but he played outfield with Babe Ruth on the Yanks from 1920 through 1929. Name him.

7. The Yankee teams of the 1920s were used to winning, but pitcher Sad Sam Jones holds the Yankee record (tied with three others) for most losses in a season. Did he lose _____ (21, 23, 24, 30) games in 1925?

FEARSOME FOES

Who are the toughest Yankee opponents, the most fearsome foes in the League?

1. True or false. The Yankees have never had a winning record against the Seattle Mariners since the Mariners were formed in 1977.

2. Which pitcher is most feared by the Bomber batters?
   a. Mike Caldwell   b. Nolan Ryan   c. Francisco Barrios
   d. Jim Palmer

3. Which American League batter bedevils Yankee pitchers, according to the pitchers themselves, more than anyone else?
   a. Sixto Lezcano   b. Rod Carew   c. Don Baylor
   d. George Brett

4. Which team boasts the best record against the Yankees in the 1977–1979 seasons?
   a. Milwaukee Brewers   b. Baltimore Orioles
   c. Seattle Mariners   d. Kansas City Royals

5. Walt Masterson is not the kind of pitcher whom young fans will remember, for he retired in 1956 after a fourteen-year career with a 78–100 record and a 4.15 ERA. But why does Mickey Mantle consider Walt to be one of the toughest pitchers he ever faced?
   a. Masterson never allowed Mantle a hit in five years of competition.
   b. Mantle could never hit curve balls which were Masterson's specialty.
   c. Masterson's awesome fastball was the most wicked Mantle had ever encountered.
   d. Mantle once struck out five times in a row against Masterson.

6. Since 1960, only one pitcher has defeated the Yankees five times in one season. Is he
   a. Luis Tiant   b. Denny McLain   c. Sam McDowell
   d. Mike Cuellar

7. His sixty career wins against the Yankees is a major league record. Who is he?
   a. Hal Newhouser   b. Walter Johnson   c. Lefty Grove
   d. Bob Feller

8. Of thirty-two World Series competitions, the Yankees have only lost ten. Which team has licked the Yanks more times than any other team?
   a. Giants   b. Dodgers   c. Cardinals   d. Braves

YANKEE TUBE TALK

Gavin MacLeod, skipper of "The Love Boat," clowns with Reggie Jackson during a break in the filming. But has Reggie ever appeared on "Hollywood Squares"?

1. When Yogi Berra was asked to choose among his favorite television shows, he loudly said:
   a. "60 Minutes"   b. "Monday Night Baseball"   c. "Gunsmoke"
   d. "I like them all."

2. He has seen plenty of squabbles and fights since he took over as Yankee owner. Therefore, it is no small wonder that George Steinbrenner considers a show about a medic unit in Korea, known as _____, his favorite show.

3. Can you match the Yankee player on the left with his favorite television show on the right?

1.	Oscar Gamble	A.	"Mork and Mindy"
2.	Bucky Dent	B.	"The Jeffersons"
3.	Elston Howard	C.	"The Love Boat"
4.	Brian Doyle	D.	"All in the Family"

4. Even though this reliever has seen enough true-life soap operas in his short Yankee career, he still prefers "One Life to Live" as his favorite television show. Is he
   a. Tom Underwood   b. Ron Davis   c. Jim Beattie
   d. Mike Griffin

5. As he works for the ABC network as a commentator on frequent occasions, it comes as no surprise that "Good Morning America" (as well as "60 Minutes") is his most watched television show. Name this outspoken outfielder.

6. True or false. Whitey Ford, a pitcher known for his sharp eye, considers Cheryl Ladd to be his favorite television actress.

KING REGGIE

1. As a college student at Arizona State University, Reggie compiled an average of
   a. A b. B c. C d. D

2. After hitting five home runs to lead the Yanks to the World Series title in 1977, Reggie Jackson told his fans:
   a. "I'm the greatest, thank you all."
   b. "Everyone helped me get where I am; now I want to help everybody have a tunafish sandwich on me."
   c. "I'm the straw that stirs the drink."
   d. "Maybe now I'm going to get the respect I've deserved."

3. For many years, Reggie's best friend on the team was
   a. Mel Stottlemyre b. Billy Martin c. Willie Randolph
   d. Fran Healy

4. Returning to Memorial Stadium in Baltimore in 1977, Reggie was greeted by Baltimore fans with
   a. hot dogs which they threw on the field.
   b. Reggie Bars which were showered into the outfield.
   c. shouts of "We love Reggie, oh yes we do!"
   d. a standing ovation.

5. Reggie has blamed his difficulties in getting along with Billy Martin on
   a. Mickey Rivers b. George Steinbrenner c. Ron Guidry
   d. the media

6. Jackson's favorite color is
   a. blue b. green c. brown d. chartreuse

7. As a mischievous child, young Reggie used to
   a. make crank phone calls.
   b. steal hubcaps.
   c. steal fruit from neighborhood grocery stores.
   d. toss mud on neighbor's car windows.

8. When Jackson won a car as MVP in the 1977 World Series, he
   a. donated it to a nursing home in Brooklyn.
   b. parked it in a Park Avenue garage.
   c. gave it as a gift to his sister, Tina.
   d. traded it in and pocketed the cash.

9. How many division championship teams did Reggie play for in the 1970s?
   a. 2   b. 3   c. 5   d. 6   e. 7

10. Reggie owns twenty-seven cars, but which one does he select as his favorite?
   a. '55 Chevy   b. white Rolls Royce   c. '38 Packard
   d. Cadillac Seville

Identify these friends of Reggie as they relax after a hard game.

True or False.

_____ **1.** Jackson was first signed by the Baltimore Orioles.

_____ **2.** One of Reggie's superstitions is that spitting at the plate helps him make contact with the ball.

_____ **3.** Reggie only wears long-sleeved shirts onto the field.

_____ **4.** Jackson says that manager Bob Lemon helped him to find "inner peace."

_____ **5.** Stevie Wonder is one of Reggie's favorite singers.

_____ **6.** Earl Weaver is the manager whom Reggie respects the most.

_____ **7.** Reggie hopes one day to own a Golden Retriever.

_____ **8.** Jackson's favorite ballpark to hit in is Fenway.

_____ **9.** Reggie endorses Fruit of the Loom underwear.

_____ **10.** Jackson plays the bongo drums for recreation.

NICKNAMES OF THE 1950S

He led American League first basemen in double plays in 1956. He was also a bruising football player in college.

Name him.

How well can you recall those golden years of the 1950s? Match the 1950s' player on the left with his nickname on the right.

1.	Whitey Ford	**A.**	Chief
2.	Frank Crosetti	**B.**	Bunky
3.	Billy Martin	**C.**	Captain
4.	Allie Reynolds	**D.**	The Chairman of the Board
5.	Hank Bauer	**E.**	Schnozz
6.	Gil McDougald	**F.**	The Crow
7.	Jerry Coleman	**G.**	Donald Duck
8.	Bill Skowron	**H.**	Moose

TRIVIA

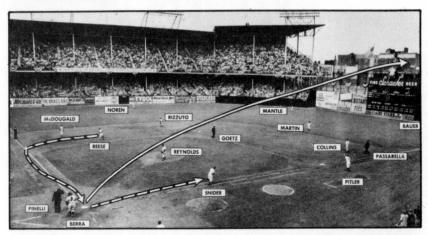

Duke Snider has just lofted one of Allie Reynolds' pitches over the right field fence in the sixth game of a hard-fought series. Was this home run hit in 1952 or 1953?

1. In 1914, Babe Ruth was signed by the Baltimore Orioles, then a minor league team. The Boston Red Sox later acquired him for a cash sum from Baltimore. What was the amount of the transaction?
   a. $250   b. $2,500   c. $25,000   d. $250,000

2. Name a former Yankee outfielder from the 1950s who became the first manager of the Oakland Athletics.

3. This former Yankee pitcher proudly hails from the Indian-dancing capital of the world, La Junta, Colorado. Who is he?
   a. Allie "The Chief" Reynolds
   b. Burleigh "Ol' Stubblebeard" Grimes
   c. Tippy Martinez
   d. William "Buffalo Bill" Hogg

4. Name a Yankee whose brother was drafted by the Green Bay Packers in 1977, played defensive back, and was later traded to the New York Jets but sat out the 1979 season on the injured reserve list.
   a. Tom Underwood   b. Doc Medich   c. Mike Griffin
   d. Willie Randolph

5. Since the institution of the Golden Glove Awards, one Yankee pitcher has won the honor four times. Who is he?
   a. Norm Siebern   b. Bobby Shantz   c. Art Ditmar
   d. Ralph Terry

6. When were Yankee fans first able to buy their tickets via telephone through the credit card CHARGIT system?
   a. 1924   b. 1968   c. 1977   d. 1980

FIND THESE YANKEES

Can you find the 22 hidden Yankees in this diagram puzzle?

```
A  O  R  E  U  G  I  F  S  S  N  R
Z  N  S  N  P  U  T  A  P  E  E  K
N  G  I  A  H  I  A  D  E  N  T  E
O  A  V  R  P  D  A  E  N  O  T  L
S  M  A  Y  L  R  K  E  C  J  L  Y
K  B  D  A  O  Y  R  P  E  Q  E  O
C  L  A  Y  D  B  B  A  R  L  S  D
A  E  X  N  N  R  S  E  N  L  M  O
J  Q  T  I  A  N  T  A  R  H  L  O
E  M  E  T  R  O  T  S  I  R  O  M
T  T  E  G  A  S  S  O  G  R  A  J
S  A  K  E  N  O  R  E  C  R  U  M
```

LOUISIANA LIGHTNIN'

1. Ron Guidry reports that his most memorable game was
   a. the playoff game against Boston in 1978.
   b. the time he struck out eighteen Angels at Yankee Stadium in June of 1978.
   c. the time he played centerfield against Toronto in 1979.
   d. his World Series win against the Dodgers in 1978.

2. In pitching nine shutouts in 1978, Guidry tied the Yankee record earlier set by
   a. Whitey Ford   b. Red Ruffing   c. Lefty Gomez
   d. Babe Ruth

3. One of the skinniest players in recent Yankee history, Guidry has a waist size of
   a. 30 – 31   b. 31 – 32   c. 32 – 33   d. 37 – 38

4. For his stellar pitching performance in 1978, Guidry won the Cy Young award unanimously. The only other unanimous winner in American League history was
   a. Jim Palmer   b. Whitey Ford   c. Denny McLain
   d. Bob Feller

5. Guidry is a man of multiple talents. In a pinch, his managers have used him as
   a. a pinch-runner because of his lightning speed.
   b. a pinch-hitter because of his ability to lay down a perfect bunt.
   c. a shortstop because of his sharp fielding finesse.
   d. a pinch-hitter because of his awesome batting power at the plate.

6. Guidry lists as his favorite television show
   a. "The Dukes of Hazzard"   b. "All in the Family"
   c. "Charlie's Angels"   d. "60 Minutes"

How well do you remember Guidry's 1978 season? Answer the following questions true or false.

_____ 7. Guidry's 248 strikeouts in 1978 led the League and surpassed the Yankee mark set by Jack Chesbro.

_____ 8. The collective batters of the American League batted only .193 against Guidry in 1978.

_____ 9. Guidry won his first thirteen games of the year, breaking the Yankee mark set by Atley Donald, the scout who had signed him.

_____ 10. Guidry's .893 winning percentage (25 – 3) was the best percentage of any pitcher in baseball history who had won at least twenty games.

NOT FOR YOUR

These candid and perhaps most revealing photos expose the Yankees in another light. Can you correctly identify any of these distorted heroes?

1

2

3

YANKEE PHOTO ALBUM

4

5

ACROSS

1 Winning or losing _____
7 Unit of work
10 Weekly church ceremony
14 Divine revelation; prophecy
15 Ballpark shout
16 *Trinity* author, Leon _____
17 Greatest Yankee switch-hitter of all time
18 "The Sultan of Swat" (two words)
20 Within: Prefix
21 Legal claim
23 Plays a role
24 Look after
25 Three, in Milan
26 Yankee catcher voted MVP in 1963
29 "When _____ do as the . . ."
33 Yankee All-Star outfielder, Hank _____
34 Woodwinds
37 Anagram for was
38 Former, as in _____ while
39 Clods or oafs
40 Unit of area for land
41 Dined

42 Pitcher Tommy _____ (He led the Yanks in saves in 1949.)
43 Walking _____ (elated)
44 Charles "King Kong" _____; outfielder with DiMaggio and Heinrich
46 Yankee outfielder who hit .326 in 1977
48 Assist
49 "_____ Lisa"
50 Chess piece or kind of shop
52 Uniting force
53 Comedian Johnson
57 "Joltin' Joe"
59 26 Across, and others
61 "So quiet you could hear _____ drop"
62 "_____ a boy!"
63 Bat Day and Old-Timers Day are special _____
64 Raced in a car
65 Expo hurler Bill _____
66 Yankee Hall-of-Fame catcher who hit .362 in 1936

32

YANKEE SLUGGERS

DOWN

1 A few
2 Transit: Abbr.
3 Fan dancer Sally _____
4 Outer: Prefix
5 Everyone
6 Yankee Hall-of-Famer Wee Willie _____ ("Hit 'em where they ain't!")
7 Receded
8 Horse color
9 Salt
10 Yankee who hit four consecutive home runs in 1970, Bobby _____
11 In _____ (fixed routine)
12 Perches
13 Library sound
19 Deserves
22 Type of pool
24 Material used in street paving
25 Evens the score
26 Author Brett _____
27 Eur. blackbird: Var.
28 Damp
30 Gamble
31 He hit his sixty-first against Stallard of Boston

32 Wide-mouthed jug
33 Bird's bill
35 Good, in Paris
36 King of the fairies, Merle _____
39 "Babe Ruth's Legs": Sammy _____ (1929–1934)
40 After prop or oct
42 Person
43 Eggs
45 "_____ order" (two words)
47 Truly
49 _____ Skowron
50 Yankee who led the League in homers in 1916 and 1917, Wally _____
51 Friend, in Lyon
52 _____ the bullet
53 Smart _____
54 Rangers' "field"
55 _____-à-tête
56 Snaky or wavy
57 German article
58 _____ McDougald
60 56, to Nero

YANKEE ETIQUETTE

Are you a well-behaved Yankee fan? Take the following test to see if your ballpark manners need improving.

1. When Lou Piniella comes to the plate, you should
   a. politely applaud. b. yell "Loooooo...."   c. yell "Boooooo...."
   d. start clapping rhythmically in unison.

2. During the seventh inning stretch, it is customary at Yankee Stadium to
   a. leave the ballpark early in order to beat the crowd.
   b. start chanting "We're Number One."
   c. review your scorecard to make sure your statistics are accurate.
   d. wave to the television cameras.

3. If you should be lucky enough to be at a pennant-winning game at the Stadium, you should
   a. dress warmly.
   b. bring fireworks and hard liquor to celebrate.
   c. cheer exuberantly when the Yankees win.
   d. run onto the field and congratulate the players.

4. If you arrive at your reserved seats and find someone already sitting there, you should
   a. ask for assistance from a friendly usher.
   b. take the nearest empty seats available.
   c. go immediately home.
   d. pour beer all over their heads.

5. When the opposing manager comes out to replace his pitcher, you as a loyal Yankee fan should
   a. begin yelling out your own suggestions as to who the next pitcher should be.
   b. begin the famous chant "It's shower time again, we're gonna miss ya."
   c. boo his presence on the mound.
   d. head for the nearest concession stand and buy a bag of freshly roasted nuts.

6. At a concession stand, a true Yankee fan would order
   a. *paté de foie gras* with a glass of white wine.
   b. a king-size hot dog and a jumbo beer.
   c. a cheeseburger with all the trimmings and a malted milk shake.
   d. soup of the day.

7. When the National Anthem is played, it is customary
   a. to head for the nearest concession stand.
   b. to salute the flag.
   c. to stand on your seat and sing along.
   d. to start cheering about two seconds before the song is over.

THE HOUSE THAT RUTH BUILT

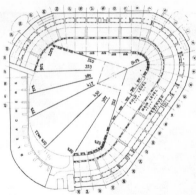

1. Opening day at Yankee Stadium was
   a. April 16, 1922   b. April 18, 1923
   c. April 21, 1924   d. Christmas Eve, 1925

2. The grounds that the present Yankee Stadium sits on were formerly part of the estate of
   a. J. P. Morgan   b. E. J. Korvette
   c. William Waldorf Astor   d. Solomon Guggenheim

3. In Babe Ruth's home run assault of 1927, he managed to sink sixty· over the outfield fences. How many of those were in Yankee Stadium?
   a. 22   b. 26   c. 28   d. 34

4. In what stadium did the Yankees play just before they debuted in Yankee Stadium?

5. Which of the following personalities have *not* played Yankee stadium?
   Pope Paul VI   The Beatles   Red Grange   Joe Lewis
   Ingemar Johansson   Douglas MacArthur   Sun Yung Moon

6. The official time-clock sign in front of the new Yankee Stadium is an advertisement for
   a. Omega   b. Timex   c. Longines   d. Bullova

7. When was the first night baseball game played at the Stadium?
   a. July 3, 1939   b. September 9, 1955
   c. May 28, 1946   d. June 31, 1947

8. Approximately how many pounds of lime are used in marking the basepaths each year?
   a. 1,000   b. 2,500   c. 4,000   d. 6,000

9. After the Dodgers' loss to the Yankees in the 1978 World Series, which infuriated Dodger player was quoted as saying: "They can drop a bomb on Yankee Stadium any time they want!"
   a. Dusty Baker   b. Steve Garvey   c. Ron Cey   d. Davey Lopes

10. Which prominent Texas university acquired the structure of Yankee Stadium in 1962?
    a. Texas A & M   b. Rice University
    c. Baylor University   d. SMU

Called the "Commerce Kid" because he hailed from Commerce, Oklahoma, Mickey Mantle is pictured here with his twin younger brothers _____ and _____.

NICKNAMES

Match the Yankee in the first column with his nickname in the second column.

1.	Joe DeMaestri	A.	Tiger
2.	Ralph Houk	B.	Poosh 'em up
3.	Billy Martin	C.	Big Cat
4.	Cliff Mapes	D.	Bullet
5.	Mickey Mantle	E.	Squatty
6.	Thurman Munson	F.	Joe's Little Bobo
7.	Tony Lazzeri	G.	Bulldog
8.	Bob Turley	H.	Major
9.	Johnny Mize	I.	The Commerce Kid
10.	Jim Bouton	J.	Oats

YANKAGRAMS

Unscramble the following anagrams and identify the ten Yankee players.

1. ENSYLGSTEACE   _ _ _ _ _
                           _ _ _ _ _ _ _

2. ZUHRIPZOITL   _ _ _ _
                            _ _ _ _ _ _ _

3. LLKYDBCEII   _ _ _ _   _ _ _ _ _ _

4. BUNTKYKEO   _ _ _ _   _ _ _ _ _

5. STEALCCKYNDREFIENH   _ _ _ _
                            _ _ _ _ _ _
                            _ _ _ _ _ _

6. LOBYRETBU   _ _ _   _ _ _ _ _ _

7. GODNEENWGOIL   _ _ _ _
                            _ _ _ _ _ _ _ _

8. WIFEDROTHY   _ _ _ _ _ _   _ _ _ _

9. SETTLERMMLOTEY   _ _ _
                            _ _ _ _ _ _ _ _

10. RAZZLETIONY   _ _ _ _
                            _ _ _ _ _ _ _

TRUE OR FALSE

_____ 1. Bucky Dent acted in a movie with the Dallas Cowboy cheerleaders in 1978.

_____ 2. Fred Stanley's foul pole home run in September 1973 was the last home run in the old Yankee Stadium.

_____ 3. Sparky Lyle has only started in one major league game.

_____ 4. The Mets have won more games than the Yankees in the Mayor's Trophy Game.

_____ 5. Ron Guidry and Whitey Ford are the only two Yankee pitchers to have two consecutive years of 200 or more strikeouts.

_____ 6. Babe Ruth was fined $5,000 and suspended in August 1925 for his lackluster performance.

_____ 7. Lou Gehrig holds the Yankee record for most RBIs in one game, eleven against the Philadelphia A's in 1936.

_____ 8. Ron Blomberg was the first Yankee to hit in the designated hitter spot in 1973.

_____ 9. Phil Rizzuto won the MVP award in 1950.

_____ 10. Joe DiMaggio batted .381 in 1939, but lost the batting title to Ted Williams.

Who is Roger Maris posing with and why?

1. Which of the following Yankee pitchers won twenty-one games for three consecutive seasons (1949, 1950, 1951)?
   a. Eddie Lopat b. Allie Reynolds c. Vic Raschi
   d. Bob Grim

2. What was Whitey Ford's overall major league winning percentage?
   a. .690 b. .701 c. .587 d. .628

3. This Yankee led the International League shortstops in double plays with ninety-one in 1966. Who is he?
   a. Dick Howser b. Bobby Murcer c. Ruben Amaro
   d. Fred Stanley

4. In which season did Mel Stottlemyre win twenty-one games (his most winning season)?
   a. 1965 b. 1966 c. 1968 d. 1969

5. Which "intellectual" Yankee, traded to the Seattle Mariners in 1979, attended Dartmouth College?

6. These two centerfielders, who have the same first name and were both speedy baserunners, share the Yankee record for fewest (two) double play grounders in one season. Name them.

7. In 1947, the Yankees combined for a winning streak of _____ (17, 19, 20, 22) games, the longest such record for the club.

TRIVIA

(Above) Gary Cooper played the lead role in the movie "Pride of the Yankees" in 1942. Whom did he portray?

(Left) Who is this man?

ARTS AND CRAFTS

Match the Yankee in the first column with his hobby in the second column.

1. Cliff Johnson   A. Raising German Shepherds
2. Reggie Jackson   B. Expensive cars
3. Graig Nettles   C. Collecting phonograph records
4. Roy White   D. Bowling
5. Sparky Lyle   E. None
6. Ron Guidry   F. Shower brawling; horseback riding
7. Chris Chambliss   G. Reading
8. Willie Randolph   H. Dancing and hunting
9. Oscar Gamble   I. Gambling
10. Mickey Rivers   J. Sitting naked on birthday cakes
11. Tommy Henrich   K. Collecting cigar boxes

12. Jugglin' Jim Bouton liked to play his off-the-field games as much as anyone. Which of the following endeavors did he occupy himself with?

    a. multiple image photography
    b. speaking Spanish on his uncle's C.B. radio
    c. designing costume jewelry
    d. training his A.K.C. poodles

THE DIMAGGIOS

Any Yankee fan can easily spot Joe, but which is Dom and which is Vince?

The questions below can all be answered by matching the brother with the correct response.

a. Joe   **b.** Dom   **c.** Vince

1. Who was the youngest?
2. Which brother never played for a New York team?
3. Which one never played a game in the infield?
4. Which one never liked linguine?
5. Which brother shared a wife in common with playwright Arthur Miller?
6. Who had the most career stolen bases?
7. Which one never hit .300?
8. Fill in the blank:
    "Where have you gone, _____ DiMaggio?"
9. Which brother never graced the American League playing fields?
10. Who of the three was *not* born in Martinez, California?
11. Which one never played in a World Series?
12. Who was the tallest?

YANKEE LOGIC

1. If it were 1964 and Whitey Ford were pitching, then who would be catching?
   a. Yogi Berra   b. Bill Dickey   c. Elston Howard
   d. Thurman Munson

2. If it were 1961 and the Yankees had just won the pennant, then over which manager's head would the players be pouring ice-cold champagne?
   a. Ralph Houk   b. Casey Stengel   c. Billy Martin   d. Yogi Berra

3. If a Yankee infield included Joe Collins at first base, Gil McDougald at second and Phil Rizzuto at shortstop, then who would be playing the hot box?
   a. Clete Boyer   b. Graig Nettles   c. Billy Martin   d. Andy Carey

4. If you were at a game where the lineup was Lefty Davis, Willie Keeler, Dave Fultz, Jimmy Williams, John Ganzel, Wid Conroy, Herman Long, Jack O'Connor and Jack Chesbro, then what major event might you have been witnessing?
   a. the first pennant-winning lineup of the Yankees
   b. the first All-Star game held in Yankee Stadium
   c. the first game ever of the New York Highlanders
   d. the first World Series win by a Yankee team

5. If you read an old newspaper which showed that the Yankees were languishing in last place at the end of September, then in which year might that paper have been printed?
   a. 1918   b. 1948   c. 1959   d. 1966

To whom does this lovely split-level home in Saddle River, New Jersey, belong? (*Hint:* He stepped down as general manager in 1966 to take over the reins of the team.)

42

FAMOUS DATES IN YANKEE HISTORY

Fill in the correct year.

1. _____ Don Larsen pitches a perfect World Series game against the Brooklyn Dodgers.
2. _____ Billy Martin catches a fly off the bat of Jackie Robinson to preserve the Yankees' World Series win against the Dodgers.
3. _____ Joe DiMaggio ends his fifty-six-game hitting streak in Cleveland.
4. _____ Mickey Mantle wins the prestigious Triple Crown.
5. _____ Ron Guidry leads the Yanks to a pennant with an amazing twenty-five-win season.
6. _____ The Yankees win their first World Championship defeating the New York Giants.
7. _____ Allie Reynolds pitches two no-hitters in one season.
8. _____ Reggie Jackson smashes three home runs in the final game of the World Series.
9. _____ Elston Howard breaks a racial barrier by becoming the Yankee's first black player.

Identify from left to right this 1937 Yankee infield, considered by many to be the best in Yankee history.

1. He batted .330 in 1935 and hit five home runs in the 1936 season. Can you name this slugging pitcher who was often used as a pinch-hitter by manager Joe McCarthy?
    a. Ernie Shaw   b. Lefty Gomez   c. Johnny Murphy
    d. Red Ruffing

2. Yankee history was made on October 20, 1931, not in Yankee Stadium, but in a small Oklahoma town. What was the cataclysmic event?

3. Put the following 1930s' events in their correct chronological order.
    a. Ted Williams gets his first major league hit, a double in Yankee Stadium, against Red Ruffing.
    b. Joe McCarthy becomes the Yankee manager.
    c. Babe Ruth hits his 700th home run against Detroit.
    d. Joe DiMaggio joins the club and bats .323 in his rookie season.

4. Babe Dahlgren batted only .235 in 531 at bats in the 1939 season, but he made history nonetheless. Can you explain this phenomenon?

5. What promotional event did the Yankees first hold at the Stadium in the 1938 season?
    a. Old-Timer's Day   b. Bat Day   c. Virgil Trucks Day
    d. Ladies' Day

6. On August 3, 1933, this veteran pitcher brought an end to the Yankees' non-shutout streak of 308 games by blanking them 7 – 0. He was:
    a. Lefty Grove   b. Monte Pearson   c. Schoolboy Rowe
    d. Dizzy Dean

7. Charlie Root won 201 games in an impressive seventeen-year career in the major leagues, but he is best remembered by New York fans for his connection to Babe Ruth. Explain.

THE 1930S

Name this feared third baseman of the Depression years.

YANKEES AND HOLLYWOOD

1. Which actor is most selected by Yankee players as their favorite movie star?
   - a. Marlon Brando   b. Clint Eastwood   c. Paul Newman
   - d. John Wayne

2. He has trouble naming his favorite movie star, because he loves all of them, and came up with a whole host of them, including Paul Newman, Robert Redford, John Wayne, Henry Fonda, Barbara Stanwyck, Bette Davis, Joan Crawford and Jimmy Stewart. Is this Yankee movie buff
   - a. Ed Figueroa   b. Ron Guidry   c. Lou Piniella
   - d. Tommy John

3. True or false.   Ron Guidry's favorite Hollywood actor or actress is Barbra Streisand.

4. Can you match the Yankee player on the left with his favorite movie star on the right?

1. Oscar Gamble	A. Al Pacino
2. Rick Cerone	B. Farrah Fawcett
3. Yogi Berra	C. John Wayne
4. Luis Tiant	D. Greer Garson

5. If Mickey Mantle were going to a drive-in movie and had his choice of seeing movies with Marilyn Monroe, Racquel Welch, Sophia Loren or Suzanne Somers, which movie would he select?

6. True or false.   Fred Stanley's favorite Hollywood actor or actress is Bette Davis.

AT THE HELM

1. Since becoming a major league manager in 1969, how many different ball clubs has Billy Martin managed?
   a. 4 b. 5 c. 6 d. 8
   Bonus. How many of these teams can you name?

2. Match the Yankee manager on the left with his nickname on the right.

1.	Casey Stengel	A.	Marse Joe
2.	Ralph Houk	B.	The Mighty Mite
3.	Miller Huggins	C.	The Professor
4.	Joe McCarthy	D.	Major

3. Johnny Keane, Bill Virdon, Bill Dickey and Bucky Harris all served at one time as Yankee managers. Can you put them in the correct chronological order of their appearance at the Yankee helm?

4. Who was the first Yankee manager to win a pennant?
   a. Joe McCarthy b. Clark Griffith c. Billy Martin
   d. Miller Huggins

5. This Hall-of-Famer, nicknamed "The Old Fox," was the first manager of the New York Highlanders back in 1903. Who is he?
   a. Kid Elberfeld b. Miller Huggins c. Joe McCarthy
   d. Clark Griffith

6. Can you select which of the following men were at one time Yankee managers?
   a. Hal Chase b. Frank Chance c. William E. Donovan
   d. Johnny Neun e. Robert Shawkey f. Harry Wolverton

7. Even though Dick Howser only played for two years as a Yankee player, he was part of a fearsome double play combination. Who played shortstop to his adroit second base?
   a. Tony Kubek b. Gene Michael c. Phil Linz
   d. Sandy Alomar

8. Of Joe McCarthy, Casey Stengel and Miller Huggins, which one had the highest winning percentage as a major league manager? Which one had the lowest?

Before he endorsed Yoo-Hoo, Yogi opened a chain of refreshment stands called The Yogi Berra Snack Bar(s). He began this venture in _____ (1950, '56, '58)?

1. Who did Yogi room with in the International League in the 1940s?
    a. Joe Garagiola   b. Bobby Brown   c. Frank Coleman
    d. Minnie Minoso   e. no one

2. Which of the following World Series records does Yogi hold?
    a. most games   b. most at bats   c. most hits
    d. most doubles

3. In the winter months of 1946 – 1947, Yogi sought extra income by working as
    a. an underwriter for Omaha Life
    b. a stock boy for Carvel
    c. a copy-editor for Scribners
    d. a groundfloorsman at Sears Roebuck
    e. a car hop for the Oasis drive-in in El Paso, Texas

4. Yogi struck out _____ times (with 550 at bats) in the 1950 season.
    a. 8 b. 12 c. 43 d. 26

5. What position did Yogi want to play when he came to the Yankees in 1946?
    a. pitcher b. catcher c. shortstop d. third base

BERRA

Name the show business personality to whom Yogi is talking.
Hint: The year is 1956.

6. While managing the slipping Yankees in August of 1964, Yogi and the now "famous" harmonica incident captured the fans' attention and brought little harmony to a pennant-contending team. Help us recall this hectic incident by filling in the blanks.

After losing ___1___ (3, 4, 5) straight to the Chicago White Sox, the downtrodden Yankees filed onto an airport bus for a flight to ___2___, an American League city in New England. Phil Linz sat in the back of the bus industriously attempting to wheeze out the simple chords of ___3___ ("London Bridge is Falling Down," "Moon River," "Mary Had a Little Lamb," "I Wanna Hold Your Hand") on his harmonica. Mr. Berra then boarded the bus and demanded that Linz take his ___4___ and to ___5___ it. Linz didn't hear Yogi and kept playing. Yogi repeated his warning which "Harmonica Boy" Linz responded to by flipping the harmonica towards Yogi and replying ___6___ ("You just don't know good music when you hear it!" "I'm just unwinding." "Do it yourself." "Blame Mel [Stottlemyre], he tol' me to do it."). The wayward throw hit Joe Pepitone in the ___7___ (head, elbow, nose, leg), and all ___8___ broke loose.

HEIGHTS AND WEIGHTS

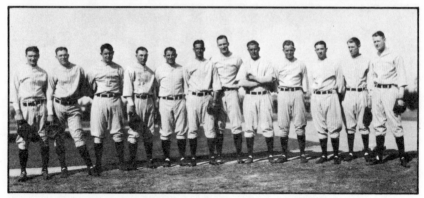

What is physically unique about this group of 1928 Yankees?

1. Who is the heaviest current Yankee?
   a. Rick Cerone b. Bob Watson c. Reggie Jackson
   d. Rich Gossage

2. Arrange the following in their descending (lightest first) order of total weight. (The weight listed in all major programs during their prime years only.)
   Hint: When arranged properly, the first initial of the first name of each will spell out a famous Yankee home run slugger.
   a. **E**nos Slaughter
   b. **B**obby Richardson
   c. **A**ndy Carey
   d. **B**ob Watson

3. Whose total weight was more: Mickey Mantle and Roger Maris or Babe Ruth and Lou Gehrig?

4. See if you can correctly identify the physical and psychic differences between two of the most famous shortstops who ever graced the Yankee infield: Phil Rizzuto and Bucky Dent.
   a. Who was taller?
   b. Who was heavier?
   c. Which one has carried more Dellwood Dairy gym bags as a promoter?
   d. His Sagitarrean nature compels him to take solitary drives in his 1957 Ford T-bird.
   e. Which one favors banana cream pie when a waitress asks "Dessert boys?"

5. Which one of these Yankees is under six feet tall?
   a. Lou Piniella b. Graig Nettles c. Bobby Murcer
   d. Tommy John

WIVES AND KIDS

1. It was a hot and sultry night in the summer of 1980. You invited the Yankees *and* their wives to a barbecue in the backyard of your Jersey home. Fill in the blanks to complete this Yankee guest list.

   a. Rich and _____ Gossage
   b. Graig and _____ Nettles
   c. _____ and Ginny Soderholm
   d. Oscar and _____ Gamble
   e. Ed and _____ Figueroa
   f. Dick and _____ Howser

   Choices: Enilda, Corna, Nancy, Eric, Juanita, Ginger

2. Doing things together is not a common Yankee tradition, but on May 5, 1980, these two Yankees became proud poppas. Who are these fathers?
   a. Ron Guidry and Oscar Gamble
   b. Bob Watson and Oscar Gamble
   c. Lou Piniella and Oscar Gamble
   d. Graig Nettles and Oscar Gamble

3. To further explore your knowledge of Yankee familial ties, match the father in the first column with the offspring in the second.
   1. Phil Rizzuto   A. Tori Keleighn
   2. Ron Guidry   B. Jamie
   3. Dick Howser   C. Tanifsha
   4. Bobby Murcer   D. Jana and Jill (twins)
   5. Willie Randolph   E. Cynthia
   6. Roy White   F. Loreena

4. Which Yankee father has a son who drank champagne and sang "We are Family" with the championship Pittsburgh Pirates of 1979?

ACROSS

1 Hall-of-Famer Williams
4 Under jrs.
9 Arabian princes: Var.
14 Past
15 Hot dog enhancer, for short
16 West Pointer
17 1978 A.L. Cy Young winner (two words)
19 _____ Root: 1912 Nobel Prize winner
20 One who keeps to himself
21 Debatable
22 _____ Paulo
23 Yankee Hall-of-Famer who was 26–5 in 1934 (two words)
28 Evergreens
29 Asparagus stalk
30 Enthrone
33 Riot gas
34 Bushel: Abbr.
37 Grow older
38 Society girl
40 Opposite of he
41 Akin to aha
42 Chris Chambliss wore this number
43 Galena and bauxite, e.g.
45 Cleveland Indians' nickname (pl.)
47 Royals' third baseman
49 Highways: Abbr.
50 Winningest Yankee pitcher (two words)
55 Home _____
56 Helper
57 _____ Mongolia
59 Debbie Reynolds Broadway role
61 "The Barber"; 1957–58 on the Yankees (two words)
65 Vex
66 Dripping sound
67 17 Across' was the lowest in the A.L. in 1978
68 Now it's a classic car
69 Demi _____ (cup)
70 Thus far

52

YANKEE HURLERS

DOWN

1 _____ Heels (North Carolina team)
2 Id partner
3 He hurled the only perfect game in World Series history
4 Skinned, to a hillbilly
5 Bay window
6 San Diego team
7 "Ben _____"
8 Pig's home
9 Red Ruffing was one
10 Swedish seaport
11 Regional dialect
12 Recultivate
13 _____ Bearcat
18 Yankee's "fire extinguisher," "_____" Gossage
22 Burn
24 Feet per minute: Abbr.
25 Rose and gunpowder, e.g.
26 Pleasure craft
27 _____ Garson is Yogi's favorite actress
28 Record achievement
31 Sun-dried brick

32 Yankee pitcher voted in 1962 the top World Series player, Ralph _____
34 A.L. Cy Young winner, 1958 (two words)
35 Actor Martin _____
36 Dan Blocker role
39 Complaint
44 Airport code for Stockholm
46 Flawed; imperfect: Abbr.
48 They dwell under bridges
50 Yankee Hall-of-Famer _____ Hoyt
51 Employed
52 Thoughts
53 Taut
54 *The Three Musketeers* author
58 Actress Sharon _____
60 Lamprey
61 Concorde, e.g.: Abbr.
62 American Philological Assn.: Abbr.
63 Wrath
64 Consume

BATTLIN' BILLY

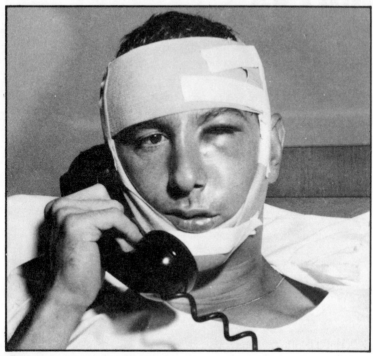

Struck in the face by Washington Senator pitcher Truman Clevenger, Billy suffered a fractured cheekbone as well as a broken jaw. What was this Washington flame thrower's nickname?

1. Always a World Series performer, Martin saved the 1952 World Series for the Yankees with his spectacular catch against the Dodgers'
   a. Jackie Robinson   b. Roy Campanella   c. Gil Hodges
   d. Duke Snider

2. In his twelve-year major league career, Martin batted
   a. .257   b. .243   c. .267   d. .249

3. On the night before Casey Stengel's funeral in Glendale, California, in 1975, Billy
   a. recalled his golden years of baseball with Mantle and Ford at Casey's house.
   b. flew to California with Yankee owner George Steinbrenner.
   c. slept in Casey Stengel's bed for the entire night.
   d. remained crying with the casket in a Glendale funeral home.

4. The simmering tension between Billy and Reggie became a full-scale battle and a national event on June 18, 1977, when
    a. Martin replaced Jackson with Ron Blomberg as a pinch hitter in the eighth inning before ABC television cameras.
    b. Martin used some foul language on Jackson on the field.
    c. Martin pulled Jackson from the game in the sixth inning for not hustling after a hit by Boston's Jim Rice.
    d. Martin publicly criticized Reggie in the locker room for his arrogance and bravado.

5. It is widely rumored that Joe DiMaggio was so upset with the theatrics at the Old-Timers Game on August 1, 1978, that he threatened George Steinbrenner that he would not return if such "incidents" were repeated. How had the great D been upstaged?

6. As a youngster in Berkeley, Billy was most taunted for his
    a. large nose   b. tattered clothes   c. large ears
    d. lack of shoes

7. Martin was fired for a second time by owner George Steinbrenner in October of 1979 after getting into a fight with
    a. a delicatessen store owner   b. Reggie Jackson
    c. Ron Guidry   d. a marshmallow salesman

THE IRON HORSE

1. "He'd be the first one dressed and on home to momma," said this Yankee veteran about Gehrig. Was he
   a. Babe Ruth   b. Joe McCarthy   c. Bill Dickey   d. Pete Sheehy

2. What was Gehrig's alma mater?
   a. Yeshiva University   b. Hebrew Union College
   c. Columbia University   d. Baruch College

3. Known as Lou and The Iron Horse, what was Gehrig's legal name?

4. She played wife Eleanor in "The Pride of the Yankees." Name this actress.

5. After this fellow player made some mildly derogatory remarks about Lou Gehrig's mother in 1933, the two men rarely spoke again. Who was he?

6. Lou Gehrig won the American League batting title _____ (1, 3, 5, 6) time(s).

7. Who was Gehrig's Yankee roommate for many years?
   a. Tony Lazzeri   b. Babe Ruth   c. Lefty Gomez
   d. Bill Dickey

·8. One of the most famous baseball pictures of the twentieth century shows a tearful Gehrig being hugged by a doleful Ruth. Can you name this momentous occasion?

9. Early in his Yankee career, Gehrig was experiencing a terrible batting slump. His mother's remedy to overcome it was
   a. three teaspoons of cod liver oil before bedtime.
   b. to eat pickled eels before a game.
   c. to chant Burma Shave jingles while driving to the ballpark from New Rochelle.
   d. a few nips of bootleg gin from Ruth's secret cache.

10. True or false. Lou Gehrig played his last All-Star game in Yankee Stadium in 1939.

11. Gehrig led the League five times in the RBI department. What was his highest total for one season?
    a. 142   b. 174   c. 192   d. 184

THE BOYER BOYS

Which Boyer brother is missing from this photograph?

How well do you remember those slick–fielding Boyer brothers? Answer Ken, Clete or Cloyd to the following questions.

1. Who was the youngest?
2. Which one was not a third baseman?
3. Which of the boys played for the Mets?
4. Who was a player representative from 1963 through 1966?
5. Who was the tallest?
6. Which one never played in a World Series?
7. Which had the nickname Junior?
8. *Trivia teaser.* Match the brother with the Missouri town he was born in.

Cloyd	Alba
Clete	Liberty
Ken	Cassville

9. Which one of the brothers batted .272 for the Yankees in 1962?
10. Who cares?

NAME THAT HERO

Here are official scorecards from famous Yankee encounters. Can you identify the hero of each of these games and the date on which history was made?

YANKEES	1	2	3	4	5	6	7	8	9	10	11	12	AB	R	H	RBI	E
Richardson	1-3		4-3			F^3		9									
Kubek				K^2		B-5		10							11		
Maris	7 D		◆		K^2		4 9								H	1	
Berra	4 9		4-3														
Lopez						D^9											
Blanchard		L^9	F^3				3u										
Howard		D^8		6-3													
Reed						3									1		
Skowron		K^2		K^2											1		
Hale						6-4											
Boyer			LD^9														
Stafford			6-3	K^2		IN 6 7											
Reniff																	
Turley																	
Arroyo																	
Tresh																	
Totals R/H	0/1	0/0	0/0	1/1	0/0	0/1	0/2	0/0						1	5	1	

BOSTON	1	2	3	4	5	6	7	8	9	10	11	12	AB	R	H	RBI	E
Schilling	K^2		5			3-6	6-3								1		
Geiger	K^2			2-3		FO SB		IN 7 8									
Yastrzemski	K^2			K_c^2	D^9			4-6							1		
Malzone		6-3		4		8		8 TL									
Clinton		K^2			9		6-3	FO 4									
Runnels		6-3			7		K^2										
Nixon			6-8				9								IT		PB
Green			D^8	←L→				K^2 ←R									
Stallard			2-3 SH	K^2													
Nichols							(6)										
Jensen																	
Totals R/H	0/0	0/0	0/1	0/0	0/1	0/1	0/0	0/0	0/1					0	4	0	

YANKEES	1	2	3	4	5	6	7	8	9	10	11	12	AB	R	H	RBI	E
Bauer	6		5-3		3 5-1-3		K²								1	1	
Collins	5-3		K²c		8	K²									1		
Mantle	7 ←L→		◆		3U									H	1	
Berra		6 IN7		8		5 F											
Slaughter		7		1-6		7											
Martin		K²		FO 6-3		6 67								1		
McDougald			5-3		6-4											
Carey			2 F		FO 6									1		
Larsen			2 F		2-4 SH	K²										
Totals R/H	0/0	0/0	0/0	1/1	0/0	1/3	0/0	0/0					29	2	5	2	0

DODGERS	1	2	3	4	5	6	7	8	9	10	11	12	AB	R	H	RBI	E
Gilliam	K²c ←L7		4-3			6-3 HARD											
Reese	K²c		4-3														
Snider	L 9		K²c			7											
Robinson		5-6-3 HARD		9		1-3										
Hodges		K²		8 HARD		5										
Amoros		4 IN9		4-3		8										
Furillo		9		4		9										
Campanella		K²c		4		4-3										
Maglie		8		K²												
Mitchell						K²										
Totals R/H	0/0	0/0	0/0	0/0	0/0	0/0	0/0	0/0	0/0				27	0	0	0	0

He never batted clean-up during his years with the Yankees, but he doesn't seem to mind the duty Uncle Sam imposed on him in his stint with the Infantry. Name this former Yankee shortstop and current sportscaster.

YANKEES	1	2	3	4	5	6	7	8	9	10	11	12	AB	R	H	RBI	E
Rivers	7		4-3	/	2-6 -9		FC -9						IIII		II		
Randolph	6-3	8		④ rc	5-3								IIII	I			
Munson	6-3	/	HR-7	8	K 2-3								IIII	I	I		PB
Jackson	/	② w	◆	◆			◆						III	IIII	HH H	IIII	
Chambliss		◆	FC ②	3U			4-3						IIII	II	HP	II	
Nettles		3U	4-3	/	K		K						IIII				
Piniella		9	SAC 7		8		3						III			I	
Dent		4-3		w		6-3		/					II				I
Torrez		/	K	6-3		/	K						III				
Totals R/H	0/0	2/1	0/0	3/3	2/2	0/0	0/1	1/1					31	8	8	8	I

DODGERS	1	2	3	4	5	6	7	8	9	10	11	12	AB	R	H	RBI	E
Lopes	6-3	/	1-3	/	7		/	3-6 -8					IIII	I			
Russell	4-3	6-3		64 w		9							III				
Smith	② P0 E6	◆	DP 6-4-3			DP 3-6-3							IIII	II	H	I	
Cey	③ w	-5		/	K		/	K					III	I	I		
Garvey	③9	8			9		F-7 ⑤6 -9 -5						IIII	I	TI	II	
Baker	K		/	9	7		-9						IIII	I			
Monday	/	3U	-7 -9		/	4-3	9						IIII	I			
Yeager		K	7-4 -9			1-3							III			I	
Davalillo							-5						I				
Hooton		9	K										II				
Sosa													I				
Rau																	
Goodson					K								I				
Hough																	
Lacy								I I									
Totals R/H	2-0/1	0/0	I/2	0/2	0/0	0/0	0/0	I/3					34	4	9	4	0

TRIVIA

1. How old was Ryne Duren in his official rookie year?
   a. 22   b. 24   c. 28   d. 32

2. As a player, he came to bat ninety-two times in his rookie season of 1947, but only batted a total of sixty-six times in his remaining seven seasons as a Yankee. Who was this player? (*Hint:* He played catcher.)

3. Which Yankee player was the first to ever hit a World Series pinch-hit home run?
   a. Mickey Mantle   b. Yogi Berra   c. Frank "Home-Run" Baker

4. Which of the following teams did Don Larsen play for after being traded from the Yankees after the '59 season?
   a. Kansas City Athletics (AL)   d. Houston Colt 45's (NL)
   b. Chicago White Sox (AL)   e. Baltimore Orioles (AL)
   c. San Francisco Giants (NL)   f. Chicago Cubs (NL)

This proud Yankee second baseman of the 1940s displays a black bear he bagged on a hunting trip. Who is he?

a. Joe Gordon
b. George Stirnweiss
c. Nick Etten
d. Charlie Keller

YANKEES	1	2	3	4	5	6	7	8	9	10	11	12	AB	R	H	RBI	E
Rivers	≡	⊤	⊤	BUNT		9								111	TN		
White	5b ss RBI	W,	W	SAC 34		3U								11	1	1	
Munson	Throw	∘ RO1	7	42x R81		K								111	11		
Chambliss	SF7 R81	4-6 R21		≡	56			≡ R81						11	DTH	111	
May	8	8	K	26 ES													
Nettles	6̂	6̂	3̂		W												
Gamble		KC	43	W	SAC 24												1
Randolph	9	3̄	W	63													
Stanley	53	W	4̄	9													
Totals R/H	2/3	0/0	2/2	0/1	2/3	0/0	0/0	1/1						7			

KANSAS CITY	1	2	3	4	5	6	7	8	9	10	11	12	AB	R	H	RBI	E
Cowens	43	43		663 DP			⊣	W						1			
Poquette	K	13		43		⊣	54							11	DH		
Brett	⊨	8		8	≡									1	3		
Mayberry	≡ 2 R81	43		⊣		43								1	HI	2	
McRae	K		3	13		7											
Quirk		7	63		3̄	K											
Rojas		⊣	7		63		63							1	1		
Patek		K		3	28		63							1			
Martinez		9		.		7	.							111	1		
Totals R/H	2/2	1/2	0/0	0/0	0/1	0/1	3/3	0/1						6			

ALMA MATERS

Match the player listed below with his college alma mater pinpointed on this Yankee map. (Note: Some players attended the same university.)

Graig Nettles   John Blanchard   Lou Piniella   Bucky Dent
Mickey Rivers   Lou Gehrig   Rich Gossage   Roy White
Jim Beattie   Red Rolfe   Reggie Jackson   Tommy John
Bobby Bonds   Jim Mason   Bob Watson   Bill Skowron

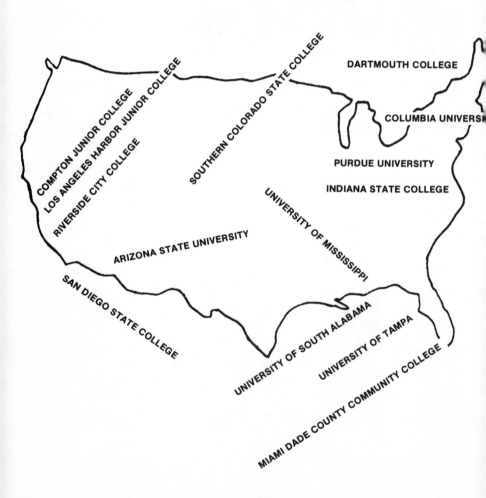

CRYPTOQUOTES

The following are ten cryptoquotes, all famous comments by New York Yankees, past and present. Break the code which applies to all the quotes and you will be able to identify the phrase and the speaker.

1. VZCPL B PM VUO HKWEBGV MPY ZY VUO DPWO ZD VUO OPTVU.
    — HZK ROUTBR

2. ZYO'G P IZTY HBPT, VUO ZVUOT'G WZYNBWVOC.
    — IBHHL MPTVBY

3. BV'G RTOPV VZ IO FBVU P FBOYOT.
    — HKBG VBPYV

4. UZHL WZF!
    — AUBH TBQQKVZ

5. B UPC P IOVVOT LOPT VUPY UO CBC.
    — IPIO TKVU

6. LZK WZKHC HZZE BV KA.
    — WPGOL GVOYROH

7. B IORROC UBM YZV VZ IKL VUPV AHPYO.
    — ROZTRO GVOBYITOYYO

8. B'M VUO GVTPF VUPV GVBTG VUO CTBYE.
    — TORRBO XPWEGZY

9. DTZM WL LZKYR VZ GPLZYPTP.
    — RTPBR YOVVHOG

10. BR APLG VZ GPNO PV VUO IZFOTL.
    — XZO CBMPRRBZ

Who is this former Yankee who insisted on being photographed in front of the centerfield monuments?
a. Matty Alou
b. Felipe Alou
c. Jesus Alou
d. Dave Kingman

THE SULTAN OF SWAT

1. What was the name of the parish house where Ruth grew up and where was it located?
2. What order were the Sisters of the parish where Ruth grew up?
3. True or False. Before leaving Boston in 1919, Ruth in the off season actually auditioned for a small role in Boston owner Harry Frazee's production of "No, No, Nanette?"
4. What was the highest batting average Ruth had as a Yankee?
5. Who played the Bambino in "The Babe Ruth Story"?
6. Who played the Sultan of Swat in "Pride of the Yankees"?
7. In what ballpark did Ruth hit his infamous "called-shot" home run?
8. What was the lowest ERA Ruth attained in a year?
9. What was Babe Ruth's legal name?
10. Which Yankee tied Babe Ruth's American League record for the most shutouts by a lefthander in a season?

Describe in twenty-five words or less what is happening in this picture.

Before an exhibition game at Wrigley Field in 1927, the Babe stood at the plate and clouted out how many home runs in one hour? There were six different pitchers throwing.

a. 38
b. 22
c. 125
d. 51

MOST MEMORABLE GAMES

No doubt you can remember your favorite game. Players, believe it or not, have their favorite games too. Try to identify the Yankee speaker, given the choice of these names.

Brian Doyle	Bobby Murcer	Reggie Jackson
Sparky Lyle	Bob Watson	Luis Tiant
Mickey Mantle	Bucky Dent	Fred Stanley
Yogi Berra	Enos Slaughter	Rich Gossage
Thurman Munson	Tommy John	Tom Underwood
Catfish Hunter	Ed Figueroa	Lou Piniella
Elston Howard	Ron Guidry	Bob Turley

_____ 1. In my first major league game, I shut out the Yankees 3-0 in 1964 as a pitcher for the Indians.

_____ 2. It was my homer in the playoff game against Boston.

_____ 3. I got the last out against Boston in the 1978 playoff game.

_____ 4. I struck out eighteen players on the Angels in one game.

_____ 5. I caught Larsen's perfect game.

_____ 6. I batted five for five against Boston in my first Yankee game in 1955.

_____ 7. I beat the Phillies 4-1 in the pouring rain to clinch the pennant for the Dodgers in 1977.

_____ 8. Sixth game, 1977 World Series, from 8:00 to 10:45, I hit three home runs.

_____ 9. I scored the 1,000,000th run in baseball in 1975 while playing for the Houston Astros.

_____ 10. My perfect game against the Twins in 1968.

_____ 11. I replaced Willie Randolph at second base and batted .438 in the 1978 Series.

THE CATFISH HUNTER STORY

1. What does Catfish have in common with Sandy Koufax and Jim Bunning?
    a. They are all righthanders.
    b. They have all starred on California teams.
    c. They have all won World Series games.
    d. All have pitched a perfect game.

2. Who once ordered Catfish to grow a mustache?
    a. Charley Finley   b. Helen Hunter
    c. George Steinbrenner   d. Billy Martin

3. As a player for the Athletics, Hunter pitched for _____ (1, 3, 4, 5) seasons before he had a winning record in one year.

4. As a boy, the young Jim Hunter tried to learn the most about pitching style from
    a. Robin Roberts and Eddie Lopat
    b. Don Larsen and Vic Raschi
    c. Warren Spahn and Lew Burdette
    d. Bob Feller and Allie Reynolds

5. In order to save money on his North Carolina farm, Catfish does the following:
    a. washes his own underwear
    b. limits himself to two meals a day
    c. only buys used cars and trucks
    d. gives his hunting dogs their shots

6. Match the pitching record on the left with the year in which Hunter achieved it on the right.

1.	12 – 15	**A.**	1975
2.	21 – 7	**B.**	1969
3.	23 – 14	**C.**	1972
4.	25 – 12	**D.**	1974

7. True or false. Hunter never won the Cy Young award.

8. Signed as a free agent by the Yanks in 1974, Hunter's total financial package came to:
    a. $1,250,000   b. $2,275,000   c. $3,750,000   d. $5,000,000

In 1946, the Yankee player on the extreme left succeeded Joe McCarthy as manager of the Yankees. He began his career as a catcher in 1928. Who is this famous backstop?

1. En route to a season of twenty-six victories, this premier hurler no-hit the Yankees, 1–0, on April 30, 1946. It was the first no-hitter against the club in twenty-seven years. Name the pitcher.
   a. Hal Newhouser   b. Bob Feller   c. Bob Lemon   d. Early Wynn

2. Why will Cookie Lavagetto always be remembered by Yankee fans as the spoiler?

3. Before being named manager of the Yankees at the end of the 1948 season, Casey Stengel had managed just previously in
   a. Brooklyn   b. Boston   c. Denver   d. Oakland

4. Nicknamed "The Big Train," this pitching great engaged Babe Ruth in a classic pitching/home run duel at the Stadium in 1942 to benefit the war bond drive. Name this great hurler who was elected to the Hall of Fame in 1936.

5. This fireballer went 20–4 and led the American League with a 1.64 ERA in 1943. He is
   a. Allie Reynolds   b. Floyd Bevens   c. Spud Chandler
   d. Ernie Bonham

6. Can you place these four events from the 1940s in their correct chronological order?
   a. Joe DiMaggio hits in fifty-six consecutive games.
   b. The Bambino dies in New York City and millions grieve.
   c. The Tigers' Fred Hutchinson shuts out the Yankees to end their record nineteen-game winning streak.
   d. Snuffy Stirnweiss' .309 batting average leads the American League.

7. His 148 games without an error is a record for a catcher. He is
   a. Bill Dickey   b. Yogi Berra   c. Ralph Houk
   d. Aaron Robinson

THE 1940S

(Above) Pictured here with his dog Dusky, he only played one season for the Yankees in the 1940s, unable to live up to his predecessor's legend. Who is he?

(Right) Identify this slick-fielding shortstop of the 40s whose talents were passed on to a young Phil Rizzuto.

8. He broke in with the 1946 Yankees and never had a winning percentage of under .677 in eight Yankee seasons. He is
    a. Allie Reynolds   b. Vic Raschi   c. Eddie Lopat
    d. Whitey Ford

9. Nicknamed "King Kong," he graced the outfield along with Tommy Henrich and Joe DiMaggio and had a lifetime batting average of .286. Who is he?
    a. George Selkirk   b. Clint Courtney   c. Charlie Keller
    d. Gene Woodling

DO JOCKS READ?

1. Turmoil apparently lies deep in the heart of this hard-throwing Southern southpaw, for he enjoys books on the Civil War. Can you name him?

2. One hundred sixty-two grueling games a year mean many lonely nights in strange hotel rooms. Which three of the following players reach for the bestseller of all time, The Bible, and call it the last book they have read?
    a. Jim Spencer   b. Sparky Lyle   c. Mickey Mantle
    d. Brian Doyle   e. Billy Martin   f. Reggie Jackson   g. Roy White

3. Which of the following Yankee hurlers has had his memoirs published in the last fifteen years?
    a. Tommy John   b. Virgil Trucks   c. Ryne Duren
    d. Whitey Ford   e. Jim Bouton   f. Sparky Lyle   g. Dock Ellis

4. He's tall, blond, stands on the hill and enjoyed parts of *Mommie Dearest* by Christina Crawford. Who is he?

5. Which book was named by the 1980 team as their most frequently read book?
    a. *Gone With the Wind*, Margaret Mitchell
    b. *Ordeal*, Linda Lovelace
    c. *The Yankee Quiz Book*, Weil and Fitzgerald
    d. *The Bronx Zoo*, Sparky Lyle

ARE YOU A YANKEE ADDICT?

TEST YOURSELF

What are the tell-tale signs of Yankee addiction? Have you been keeping Yankee yearbooks and scorecards secretly stashed in the bottom drawer of your bedroom bureau? Does your speech become slurred or your driving impaired on days when the Yankees lose? Answer the following fifteen questions truthfully to determine the extent of your addiction to the Yankees.

1. Do you go to Yankee games alone?
    a. You don't go to Yankee games at all.
    b. You only go to games with your friends or family.
    c. You have gone to games alone during dark moods.
    d. You've never missed a home game and even on rainy days you hang around the Stadium, just in case.

2. How does your weekly time spent listening or watching Yankee games compare with the same period last year?
    a. less time than last year
    b. about the same
    c. somewhat more than last year
    d. substantial increase over last year

3. Do you conceal the extent of your Yankee involvement from family or friends?
    a. never
    b. on some occasions
    c. often
    d. all the time

4. How often do you have flashbacks to Bucky Dent's playoff home run in Boston, Reggie Jackson's three-home-run Series game, or Chris Chambliss' pennant-winning clout against Kansas City?
    a. You couldn't be bothered with such nonsense.
    b. You recall the events if they are brought up.
    c. You discuss them often with friends.
    d. You are obsessed in your dreams and daydreams with these events.

5. Have there been any times in the last three years when you went for at least a month without thinking about the Yankees?
    a. You never think about the Yankees, anyway.
    b. You easily forget the Yankees during the off-season.
    c. a few times
    d. You can't put the Yankees out of your mind.

6. If you're in a candy store, how frequently do you, after careful consideration, buy a Reggie Bar?
    a. never
    b. You've bought them a few times.
    c. frequently
    d. They are a major part of your daily diet.

7. Do you save Yankee baseball cards, yearbooks, and other such memorabilia?
    a. You've never gone in for such stuff.
    b. only as a kid
    c. You like to collect and show all your house guests your treasures.
    d. If your house were burning down, your Yankee keepsakes would be the first things you'd save.

8. Have you ever missed work or school to watch the Yankees play?
    a. never
    b. once in a while
    c. often during the baseball season
    d. Work or school is always secondary to your involvement with the Yankees.

9. On nights when the Yankees lose, how often do you have sex?
    a. all the time
    b. occasionally
    c. infrequently
    d. never

10. Would you name your children or pets after Yankee players?
    a. no
    b. You have never done so, but would consider naming your new puppy Casey.
    c. After taking this quiz, you plan to name your children or grandchildren after the players.
    d. You already have a daughter named Micki and two sons named Bucky and Whitey.

11. Do you get irritable when the Yankees lose?
    a. never
    b. You are annoyed, but not irritable.
    c. Yes, but you do not become violent.
    d. You have been known to destroy your Yankee furniture and kick your pets after losses.

12. How often do you buy products endorsed by Yankee players?
   a. You've never done so.
   b. As a child, you drank Yoo-Hoo and used Bryllcream, but as an adult, you resist such temptations.
   c. You'd consider keeping your money at the Bowery, but you're no Yankee product fanatic.
   d. You keep *all* your money at the Bowery, eat *only* Yankee Franks endorsed by Luis Tiant, wear *only* Murjani jeans plugged by Reggie, and wallpaper your *entire* living room with Bucky Dent posters.

13. Have you ever tried to cut down on your Yankee addiction?
   a. You're not interested in the team in the first place.
   b. You are a steady fan, but your addiction has not gotten out of hand.
   c. You have trouble cutting down and may want to seek help.
   d. You are already a member of Yankees Anonymous.

14. Do you make it a point to memorize Yankee baseball statistics?
  a. no
  b. You know a few important statistics, like the fact that Maris hit sixty-one home runs in 1961.
  c. You are secure, but not obsessed, in your knowledge of Yankee statistics.
  d. You are a fanatic. You know that Joe Pepitone won the Golden Glove award in 1966 and that Red Ruffing was the first Yankee pitcher to hit a grand slam in 1933.

15. Have you ever missed meals because of your interest in the Yankees?
  a. never
  b. once in a while, if an important game is on television
  c. Sometimes, but you always grab a sandwich or beer later on.
  d. On game days you fast until the outcome of the game. Victories call for the "wolfin'" down of at least a dozen Yankee Franks.

HOW TO RATE YOURSELF

Give yourself: 0 points for each time you answered a.
                   1 point for each answer of b.
                   2 points for each answer of c.
                   3 points for each answer of d.

0 – 10

You should not be reading this book. Either you are a Yankee hater, you reside in Boston, or you are a complete dud. A recommended course of action would be to tune in to more Yankee games or attend them in person.

11 – 20

You are a Yankee fan of some moderation. You should not be worried about becoming an addict. You can continue at your present pace.

21 – 30

You are a loyal Yankee fan and have an abiding interest in the team. But you may be on the road to addiction. Monitor your behavior carefully, watch for those tell-tale signs and take this test again next year.

31 – 40

You are an intensely involved fan. Your interest in the team may have already begun to interfere with your work or your family life. You may be on a collision course with Yankee addiction. You may even have to seek professional help.

41 – 45

Without a doubt, you are a confirmed Yankee addict. You cannot live without the Bronx Bombers and have let the team take over your life. The road to normalcy is long and difficult, but is it really worth it?

BOMBER BOSSES

Name these 1973 chieftains.

1. Owners Frank Farrell and Bill Devery brought the first American League franchise to New York City and called their team the Highlanders. How much did they pay for the team that they "stole" from Baltimore?

   a. $18,000   b. $180,000   c. $1,800,000   d. $18,000,000

2. Perhaps the most famous of Yankee owners, Colonel Jacob Ruppert reigned as Bomber boss from 1915 until his death in 1939. He had originally paid $460,000 for the team, but how did he make his first fortune?

   a. in the shipbuilding business
   b. in railroads
   c. in beer
   d. in fast-food fried chicken franchises

3. This Yankee general manager in the 1950s was known for his strict rules, small pocketbook and no-nonsense attitude. He once put a lady detective on the trail of handsome pitcher Joe Page who he believed was not keeping curfew. Who is this general manager?

   a. Al Rosen   b. Cedric Tallis   c. Lee MacPhail   d. George Weiss

4. Owner George Steinbrenner made a smart move by naming this man general manager. He acquired, through farsighted trades, some of the most valuable Yankees of the 1970s, including Sparky Lyle, Graig Nettles, Lou Piniella, Ed Figueroa and Mickey Rivers. Name this wheeler-dealer.

   a. Gabe Paul   b. Gene Michael   c. Cedric Tallis
   d. Al Rosen

YANKEE ALL-STARS

This is a remarkable photo of the 1937 American League All Stars, as every player here, though not all of them Yankees, has made the Hall of Fame. Can you recall these seven legends?

1. His 0-1 record and 21.00 ERA in three All-Star games does not make him the envy of other pitchers. Name this Yankee reliever.
   a. Bobby Shantz   b. Johnny Murphy   c. Rich Gossage
   d. Sparky Lyle

2. Six Yankee players, Ben Chapman, Bill Dickey, Lou Gehrig, Lefty Gomez, Tony Lazzeri, and of course Babe Ruth, all made the All-Star team in 1933. What made the event something special that year?

3. He is the only Yankee to have hit a home run at Yankee Stadium, in 1939, in All-Star competition. Is he
   a. Frank Crosetti   b. Joe Gordon   c. Lou Gehrig
   d. Joe DiMaggio

4. Always a clutch player, he was selected to play in nine All-Star games between 1969 and 1979, and has come through with an impressive .300 batting average and one home run. Name this premier Yankee.

5. This ace-fielding infielder was chosen to play on seven All-Star teams in the late 1950s and early 1960s. Can you name him from these choices?
   a. Moose Skowron   b. Bobby Richardson   c. Gil McDougald
   d. Joe Pepitone

6. Joe DiMaggio, Yogi Berra and Mickey Mantle have been selected for more All-Star teams than any other Yankee players. Which of these three was selected for the most number of years? Which for the fewest?

7. In what year was the last All-Star game held at Yankee Stadium?
   a. 1978   b. 1977   c. 1975   d. 1960

MICKEY THE MAGNIFICENT

1. In an eighteen-year career, Mantle was selected to play for how many All-Star teams?
   a. 12 b. 16 c. 17 d. 18

2. Mutt Mantle, a baseball lover, named his son Mickey after which baseball great?

3. What was Mickey's favorite baseball superstition?
   a. He only wore long-sleeved shirts on the field.
   b. He would step on first base while coming on and off the field.
   c. He would spit on home plate frequently.
   d. He would keep a rabbit's foot in his back pocket while playing a game.

4. According to Mantle, who were the three toughest pitchers whom he faced in his career?
   a. Hoyt Wilhelm/Sandy Koufax/Juan Marichal
   b. Walt Masterson/Bob Feller/Denny McLain
   c. Sandy Koufax/Walt Masterson/Don Drysdale
   d. Hoyt Wilhelm/Bob Feller/Sandy Koufax

5. Mantle's favorite current television show is
   a. "WKRP in Cincinnati" b. "60 Minutes" c. "The Gong Show"
   d. "All in the Family"

6. What was Mickey's salary for the 1952 season?
   a. $7,500 b. $9,500 c. $11,000 d. $18,900

7. The lineup in the Yankee outfield in 1951 consisted of DiMaggio, Mantle and Jackie Jensen. Which position did each of them normally play?

8. Which, according to Mantle, is his most memorable game?
   a. the seventh game of the 1958 World Series against the Braves
   b. the game in which Maris hit his sixty-first home run
   c. Don Larsen's perfect game
   d. the game in 1955 in which he slugged three homers

9. How many times did Mantle lead the American League in home runs?
   a. 3 b. 4 c. 6 d. 7

10. Mantle's total of 1,710 _____ places him as Number 1 in the American League in this category of baseball.

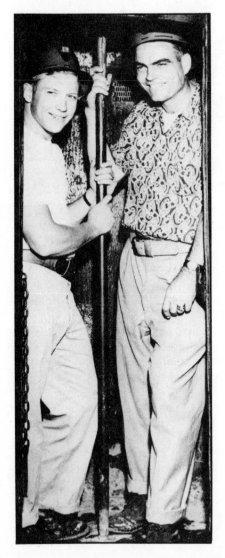

True or False.

_____ 1. Mantle's favorite movie actress is Sophia Loren.

_____ 2. Mantle's 536 career home runs place him sixth on the all-time list.

_____ 3. Billy Martin was Mickey's Yankee roommate in the early 1950s.

_____ 4. Mantle was the first player to congratulate Maris when Maris hit his sixty-first home run.

_____ 5. Mantle has been the only Yankee captain besides Lou Gehrig and Thurman Munson.

_____ 6. Mantle's eighteen home runs in World Series competition is second only to Babe Ruth.

Name the year in which a "daring" Mickey and veteran outfielder Cliff Mapes prepare to descend 300 feet down the shaft of the lead and zinc mines of Commerce, Oklahoma.

SERIES TALK

Lou Piniella, Catfish Hunter and Ron Guidry are shown here celebrating their team's victory in the fourth game of the 1978 Series. But which pitcher won the game?

Here are some of the most famous World Series quotes. We'll give you the name of the speaker as well as the opposing team; you supply the year, in the space provided.

_____ **1.** "Great game Don [Larsen]!" Yogi Berra's comment after Larsen's perfect game against the Brooklyn Dodgers.

_____ **2.** "Oh, geez, there goes three . . . four thousand dollars." Willie Mays lamenting his team's defeat.

_____ **3.** A sportswriter said after this contest against the Chicago Cubs about Babe Ruth: "Then he [Babe] put up one finger, saying I got one left. And then he pointed to direct centerfield. He hit that pitch right into what must have been a sixty-mile-an-hour wind coming off that lake and I don't know how he did it."

_____ **4.** "They stood and cheered and cheered. It rocked ol' Ebbets Field forever." A fan remarking about the first of the famous subway series with the hated Brooklyn Dodgers.

_____ **5.** "How's Tony [Kubek]?" asked a concerned Mickey Mantle after Kubek had sustained a throat injury off the wicked bat of Pittsburgh's mean Gino Cimoli.

_____ **6.** Reflecting on his game-winning catch, Billy Martin related, "I was thinking about Yogi. I was afraid he'd be coming out for the ball and sometimes when he did, he kept on his mask." The Dodgers had fallen victim to the Yankees again.

STENGELESE

Casey Stengel spoke an often incomprehensible language all his own. Translate the following Stengelese phrases into proper English.

1. He can pinch off your earbrows.
   _____

2. Tell the writers that I'm being embalmed.
   _____

3. He's throwin' worm killers.
   _____

4. A ball park that holds heat very well.
   _____

5. You put the whommy on him but, when he's pitchin', the whommy tends to go on vacation.
   _____

   _____

6. I never could done it without my players.
   _____

7. I wasn't born old.
   _____

8. Wuz you born in Poland?
   _____

9. The doctors say it don't hut none if I shake my arm once in a while and wear the cast to bed, but to watch out I don't drop it on Edna so maybe this should be the time she sits up watching me sleep all night like she does when I'm sick cause she cares about me which some of you gentlemen, if you listen to the Yankees some years back, would hardly believe.
   _____
   _____
   _____
   _____
   _____

   _____

10. You could look it up.
    _____

AS THEY WERE THEN

We tend to forget that one is not born a Yankee.
See if you can identify these players in their pre-Yankee years.

1

Co-captain of his fifth grade basketball team, he later moved on to baseball. He hit thirty-three home runs in 1962.

(Below) The "Commerce Comet" obviously gained some of his good looks from his dad.

2

(Left) As a twenty-year-old bonus baby he has just received a check for $85,000 to play baseball.

3

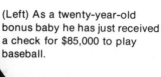

4

(Above) A baseball player all his life, he holds the record for pitching for the Yankees for the most years.

(Right) He had plenty of time to fish in those early years in Kentucky. This hard-throwing left-hander played from 1964 through 1969 with a then unimpressive Yankee team and is best remembered for his "folly floater."

5

ACROSS

1 "Golden _____" Brown
4 Type of steak
9 To _____: (no exceptions)
13 *Much _____ About Nothing*
14 Medieval lyrics
15 Jim _____ (only Yankee to homer in 1976 World Series)
17 Marsh
18 Hall-of-Famer who managed the Yanks from 1931–46 (two words)
20 Lake near which the Indians play
22 Yankee shortstop who was A.L. Rookie of the Year in 1962
23 Soft French cheese
24 Popeye's foe
26 Allocates
28 Nickname of 34 Down
32 Islamic sacred text
33 There are six in an inning
34 Celtic sea god
37 Not theirs
38 Dunes or beaches
40 After flag or foul
41 Mrs. in Mexico
42 Kind
43 Linger
44 Manager who guided the Yanks to five straight World Championships (two words)
47 Benchwarmer's milieu
50 How "The Scooter" acts when the Bosox win!
51 Even: German
52 Black
55 Yankees' home field: 1974–75
58 Yankee Hall-of-Famer who hit safely in fifty-six consecutive games
61 Hall-of-Famer Ruffing
62 Ands
63 Tendency
64 Gershwin or Thomas
65 Duration
66 Savard of the Canadiens
67 A place to work out in winter

YANKEE HALL-OF-FAMERS

DOWN

1 Ruth
2 Scent
3 Hall-of-Famer who holds the record for most World Series hits (seventy-one) (two words)
4 _____ Mahal
5 Totally drunk
6 Titania's husband
7 Appellation
8 Escapes: Abbr.
9 M.D.'s union
10 Agate
11 Houston player
12 Kind of game Don Larsen hurled in the '56 World Series
16 Pheasant broods
19 Graphs
21 Walt _____ Disney
25 Vase
27 Lifesaving service: Abbr.
28 Boxer's stats
29 Before glass or hand
30 Type of comb

31 Mandolin's cousin
34 Hall-of-Famer who played in 2,130 consecutive games (two words)
35 Or _____
36 Rod's partner
38 Farm _____ (minor leagues)
39 Roddy McDowell played one
40 Uniform part
42 It follows sigma
43 "The Princess and the _____"
44 Large Andean bird
45 Los Angeles pitcher Bill _____
46 Attempting
47 _____ vu
48 U-shaped fastening device
49 Many Gossages?
53 Gets up to the plate
54 Man-eating monster
56 Homophone of 20 Across
57 Eve's partner
59 Suffix for national or patriot
60 Poem

MOONLIGHTING

1. His cool and collected personality made him at one time a natural endorser of Kool cigarettes. He is
   a. Billy Martin b. Pedro Ramos c. Elston Howard
   d. Roy White

2. Can you match the Yankee in the left column with the product he has endorsed in the right?

1. Catfish Hunter	A.	Jockey shorts, Yoo Hoo
2. Bucky Dent	B.	Getty Oil, Murjani jeans
3. George Steinbrenner	C.	Miller Lite
4. Yogi Berra	D.	Fur coats
5. Reggie Jackson	E.	Fruit of the Loom, Chapstick

Identify the Yankee and the product that he sponsored from the following quotes:

3. "A little dab'll do ya'."
4. "It pays to save at the Bowery."
5. "It's great to be with a wiener!"

(Above) After thirteen successful seasons with the St. Louis Cardinals, this country boy came to New York and proved to be an effective pinch-hitter for the Yankees in the 1950s. Shown here in his jewelry store in the off-season, his new Yankee salary must not have disagreed with him. Name him.

(Left) Who is this muscle-bound outfielder of the 50s who kept his muscles in shape during the off-season working as a pipe fitter for the Kansas City Fire Department?

YANKEE WHEELS

Famous men need their chariots for transportation. Match the names of the following Yankees with the gas guzzlers they drive.

Choices: Rudy May, Oscar Gamble, Jim Spencer, Phil Rizzuto, Bucky Dent, Whitey Ford

THE SCOOP ON SCOOTER

1. As an enterprising young man in the 1950s, Rizzuto owned a number of bowling alleys with teammate
   a. Virgil Trucks   b. Joe DiMaggio   c. Ralph Houk
   d. Yogi Berra

2. Rizzuto's 149 career _____ places him at Number 8, between Horace Clark's 151 and Tony Lazzeri's 147, in this all-time Yankee category.

3. Philip Francis Rizzuto was born on September 25, 1918, in
   a. Bayonne, New Jersey   b. Newark, New Jersey
   c. Hoboken, New Jersey   d. New York City

4. Before becoming a Yankee broadcaster, Rizzuto announced games for the
   a. Baltimore Orioles   b. New York Mets
   c. Detroit Tigers   d. no other team

5. The Scooter hit _____ (38, 83, 122, 135) home runs in his major league career of thirteen years.

6. His 200 hits and .324 batting average garnered him the coveted MVP award in
   a. 1947   b. 1948   c. 1950   d. 1953

7. *Trivia teaser.* During his thirteen-year career as a Yankee, Rizzuto played 1,647 games at shortstop and two games at one other position. Was it
   a. catcher   b. pitcher   c. third base   d. second base

HOME RUN FEVER

1. There are five Yankee players whose career home run totals place them in the top twenty-five players on the all-time list. How many can you name?

2. He is the only Yankee to have hit four home runs in one game. Name this Hall-of-Famer.
   a. Joe DiMaggio   b. Lou Gehrig   c. Mickey Mantle
   d. Babe Ruth

3. Three Yankees have hit two home runs in one inning. Joe DiMaggio accomplished the feat in 1936, his rookie year, while another Joe, Joe Pepitone, also slugged two homers in 1962, his rookie year. But the third Yankee was neither a Joe nor a rookie when he matched the feat in 1977. Who is he?
   a. Lou Piniella   b. Thurman Munson   c. Reggie Jackson
   d. Cliff Johnson

4. Which Yankee catcher hit back-to-back pinch hit home runs in 1961?
   a. John Blanchard   b. Elston Howard   c. Yogi Berra
   d. Jake Gibbs

5. *For experts only.* Can you recall the first baseman whose low total of twenty-two home runs led the American League in 1944?

6. Of still active players, he leads the Yankees in career grand slams. Who is he?

7. During his famous fifty-six-game hitting streak in 1941, Joe DiMaggio hit _____ (8, 11, 12, 15) home runs.

Hitting a home run completely out of Yankee Stadium is a feat many a strong man has tried, but none has succeeded. The closest blast came off _____'s bat as shown here in this satellite launched off Kansas City's Bill Fischer.

8. His twenty-three career grand slams lead both the Yankees and the major leagues in this category. Name this slugger.

9. This pitcher from the early 1960s holds the dubious distinction of giving up the most home runs during a season, forty in 1962, of any Yankee hurler. Who is he?
   a. Rollie Sheldon   b. Jim Bouton   c. Ralph Terry
   d. Bud Daley

10. *Trivia teaser.* Only one Yankee, who played a mere six games for the team in 1966, hit a four-bagger in his first major league at bat. Name him.

This is perhaps the most famous four-bagger in Yankee history. Name the record that is being set.

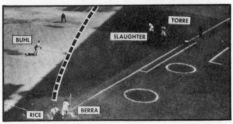

Yogi strokes another World Series home run against Milwaukee's Bob Buhl. But the home run was not the record set that game by Yogi. What was?

YANKEE LOGIC

Sample: Roger Maris is to 1961 as Babe Ruth is to

a. 1920 b. 1927 c. 1930 d. 1948

The correct answer is b. Roger Maris set his home run record in 1961, while Babe Ruth set his record of sixty in 1927.

1. Reggie Jackson is to Billy Martin as Babe Ruth is to
a. Joe McCarthy b. Jacob Ruppert c. John McGraw
d. Miller Huggins

2. Mickey Mantle is to Bobby Murcer as Joe Garagiola is to
a. Kenny Clay b. Bobby Brown c. Yogi Berra
d. Graig Nettles

3. Dick Howser is to Mike Ferraro as Ralph Houk is to
a. Phil Rizzuto b. Jerry Neudecker c. Ron Luciano
d. Frank Crosetti

4. Lou Gehrig is to 1934 as Mickey Mantle is to
a. 1951 b. 1956 c. 1967 d. 1969

5. Bob Feller is to Hoyt Wilhelm as Don Larsen is to
a. Allie Reynolds b. Spud Chandler c. Al Downing
d. Hal Reniff

6. 1960 is to 1964 as Casey Stengel is to
a. Elston Howard b. Ralph Houk c. Johnny Keane
d. Yogi Berra

7. 1977 is to Sparky Lyle as 1939 is to
a. Waite Hoyt b. Eddie Lopat c. Johnny Murphy
d. Pete Mikkelsen

TOMMY JOHN

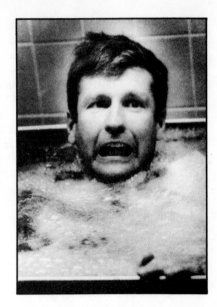

1. As a teenager, Tommy earned $30 a week by
   a. driving a beer delivery truck.
   b. working on a doughnut route.
   c. laboring in a stone quarry.
   d. helping out at his father's insurance company.

2. Which one of the following books would you most likely find on Tommy's bookshelf?
   a. *Valley of the Dolls*
   b. *They Call Me Assassin*
   c. *Oliver Twist*
   d. *RN: The Memoirs of Richard Nixon*

3. What does John have in common with pitchers Jerry Koosman, Ferguson Jenkins and Gaylord Perry?

4. John lists his most memorable baseball game as
   a. the playoff game against Boston in 1978.
   b. the time he struck out thirteen Cincinnati Reds in August 1972.
   c. the 1977 playoff game in which he defeated Philadelphia 4 – 1 to win the pennant.
   d. the two-hit shutout which he pitched at Fenway in May of 1979.

5. What does John describe as his most important career goal?
   a. to win 200 games
   b. to have a lifetime ERA of under 3.00
   c. to win a World Series with the Yankees
   d. to play for twenty years in the major leagues

6. John graduated _____ (1st, 2nd, 5th, last) in a graduating class of 225 from high school.

1. When Enos "Country" Slaughter was traded from the Cardinals to the Yankees in 1954, his first reaction was to
   a. cry and threaten to retire.
   b. say, "This is the dream of my life come true."
   c. say, "I never did like St. Louis."
   d. say, "It's a hell of a way to treat a player who's been with a team for fifteen years."

2. Which Yankee player struck the Indians' Herb Score in the face with a wicked line drive in 1957, thus bringing about an early end to the career of the "next Bob Feller"?
   a. Billy Martin   b. Moose Skowron   c. Mickey Mantle
   d. Gil McDougald

3. Edward Jones, while never a player, triggered an incident that made Yankee history in 1957. Can you name the famous brawl which made him famous?

4. Over 93,000 fans jammed the Los Angeles Coliseum in 1959 to watch the Yankees defeat the Dodgers and Sandy Koufax. What was the occasion?
   a. the first major league baseball game played on the coast
   b. the seventh game of the Dodger-Yankee World Series
   c. a benefit to aid Roy Campanella and his family
   d. the first West Coast night game, played during the exhibition season

(Left) Name this man who sat on the edge of the dugout and smoked big cigars in the 1960s, but who caught smoking fastballs in the 1950s.

THE 1950S

What year was this team photo taken?

5. The Boston Braves could no longer "pray for rain" when they traded this pitcher to the Yankees in 1951 in return for $50,000 and Lew Burdette. Name him.

6. Can you put these events from the 1950s in their correct chronological order?
   a. Billy Martin is unloaded to Kansas City in a bitterly resented move.
   b. Don Larsen hurls a perfect game in Series competition.
   c. Allie Reynolds tosses two no-hitters in one season.
   d. Bob Turley stars as a reliever, as the Yankees come from behind to defeat Milwaukee in the World Series.

7. True or false. Virgil Trucks executed a no-hitter against the Yankees in 1952.

Name these big bats from the 1950s.

HALL-OF-FAME YANKEES

Twenty-four Yankee players, managers and owners have been elected to baseball's prestigious Hall of Fame. Unscramble the names of these ten Yankee Hall-of-Famers.

1. F F R R U E G I D N
2. B O R A G E R Y I
3. S N U G G L E R L I M I H
4. D R Y O F T H E I W
5. F O G E Y M L E Z T
6. C A R R Y L A M P A H I L
7. B R O C K H J E S A C
8. S C E L A R M O B E
9. E E E E E E L L L I I W W R K
10. G H O U L G R I E

ONE LATE NIGHT AT THE COPA...

Fill in the blanks and retell the story of one of the most famous of Yankee brawls.

At 10 East 60th Street in Manhattan was located the ___1___, one of New York's most well-known nightclubs. It was a favorite haunt of ___2___ ballplayers, but in the wee morning hours of May 16, ___3___ (1956, '57, '58, '60) it would become the scene of a big brawl that would end up one month later in the trading of ___4___, the Yankee second baseman, to the ___5___ Athletics.

Following two or three drinks and dinner at Danny's Hideaway and the Waldorf Astoria, a group consisting of Yogi Berra, Whitey Ford, Mickey Mantle, Hank Bauer, Johnny Kucks and ___6___, whose birthday they were celebrating, decided to catch the late show of Sammy ___7___, Jr., then a young black entertainer, at the Copacabana. Intent on listening to the show, the players, especially Hank Bauer, were distracted by the racial taunts hurled at Sammy Davis, Jr., by an overweight delicatessen store ___8___. Bauer, one of the strongest men in the game, told the heckler, "Why don't you guys just shut up or get out." A fight quickly ensued, but Bauer denied ever hitting the man as his arms were being pinned back by catcher ___9___. Upon investigation, Bauer guessed that if anyone had hit the troublemaker, it must have been the club's ___10___. In any case, pitcher ___11___ paid the check of $84, but not before gossip ___12___, Leonard Lyons of the *New York* ___13___ got wind of the story. The next day's ___14___ ran, "Yankees Brawl in Copa."

Yankee owner ___15___ was none too pleased with the publicity. He and general manager ___16___ ordered fines of $1,000 apiece to be levied on five of the players, and $500 against the pitcher ___17___, who was making less money than the rest. To add to the bitter sting, the stout deli man had his ___18___ file a $250,000 ___19___ against the Copa and Hank Bauer. The charge was thrown out of ___20___ by a grand jury, but scrappy second baseman ___21___ had incurred the final wrath of George Weiss, who had always felt that he was a bad influence on outfielder ___22___ and the rest of the team. As a result, Martin was traded on June 15, in a move which permanently severed the warm father-son relationship between manager ___23___ and the young "brawling" Martin.

ANOTHER BRONX ZOO

Fill in the blanks and name the Yankees who own these pets.

Sparky Lyle never did tell about the real pets that his former teammates owned, but the Yankees do indeed own an impressive menagerie. As a team, the players own ____1____ (24, 28, 34, 37) dogs, but if you subtract the twenty-five pooches housed by retired pitcher ____2____ on his North Carolina farm, you would find only twelve dogs left in the Yankee kennel.

The smallest dog, a featherweight Chihuahua, is owned by husky first baseman ____3____, while fellow infielder ____4____, known for his cool wits and steady plays, keeps a Doberman Pinscher at his New Jersey home. Even lanky pitcher ____5____, whose blazing fastball would scare off any intruder, keeps a trusted German Shepherd by his side. But there are some Yankees who go in for exotica. If you rang the doorbell at the Dallas home of retired slugger ____6____, you might find a Samoyed and a Silky Terrier nipping at your heels. Not to be outdone, Cleveland tycoon ____7____ has a Bichon Frise bring his slippers to his bed.

While yelping hounds predominate, there are some other kinds of pets. Veteran pitcher ____8____, who was with the Expos in 1979, owns a spider, while ____9____, a pitching great who had his best years with the Twins and who was released by the Yankees in early 1980, raises sheep. Former Dodger ____10____, whose pitching arm has lived through several lives, enjoys the nine-lived variety and keeps a Siamese cat at his house.

____11____, always one up on his fellow teammates, owns no pets at present but plans to buy some thoroughbred horses.

Jim Bouton and his dog Pepper pose outside his Ridgewood, New Jersey, home.

TRUE OR FALSE

Catfish Hunter relaxes at his Hertford home with his hunting dog Rascal.

In a somber moment, Joe Pepitone stretches out with his poodle Fifi.

FAMOUS DATES IN YANKEE HISTORY

Fill in the correct year.

1. _____ Chris Chambliss strokes a dramatic ninth-inning home run to give the Yankees their first pennant in twelve years.

2. _____ Reggie Jackson miraculously survives a scuffle and shooting incident on Manhattan's perilous Upper East Side.

3. _____ Babe Ruth is purchased from the Boston Red Sox by owner Jacob Ruppert.

4. _____ Billy Martin resigns in mid-season in a teary farewell in Kansas City.

5. _____ Managers Johnny Keane and Ralph Houk lead the team to a tenth-place finish, its worst showing in over fifty years.

6. _____ Lou Gehrig voluntarily removes himself from the lineup after playing in 2,130 consecutive games.

7. _____ Casey Stengel is named manager of the Yankees to the amazement of fans and press alike.

8. _____ Mel Stottlemyre is brought up after mid-season and leads the team to a pennant with an impressive 9 – 3 record.

9. _____ The Yankees lose the World Series. Tony Kubek is hit on the Adam's apple by a wicked grounder and Bill Mazeroski unloads his game-winning home run.

10. _____ A stunned crowd pays farewell to Thurman Munson with an eight-minute standing ovation.

YANKEES WHO DOUBLED AS METS

1. Not only was he a player for both the Yankees and Mets, but he also led both teams to pennant victories as a manager. Name this Hall-of-Famer.

2. He broke in with the Yankees in 1955 and closed out his career as one of the fabled characters of the 1962 and 1963 Mets. Who is this marvelous New York outfielder who plugs beer on local television?

3. He played unhappily under Billy Martin in Texas, did not get along with Billy when Martin joined the Yankees in 1975, and must have been nervous when rumor had it that Martin would manage the Mets in 1979 and 1980. Who is this player?
   a. Doc Medich   b. Dock Ellis   c. Ray Burris
   d. Elliott Maddox

4. One of the great Yankee outfielders of the 1950s, he closed out his seventeen-year career by batting .274 with the 1962 Mets. Is he
   a. Gene Woodling   b. Gil McDougald   c. Sandy Alomar
   d. Tom Sturdivant

5. Nicknamed Supersub, he played a great shortstop for the Yankees beginning in 1962, but had trouble hitting for both the Mets and Yanks. Who is this player who retired from the Mets in 1968?
   a. Bud Harrelson   b. Phil Linz   c. Ed Kranepool
   d. Ed Charles

6. This outfielder batted .400 in the 1969 World Series, but was traded two years later to the Yankees. Who is he?
   a. Cleon Jones   b. Tommy Agee   c. Ed Kranepool
   d. Ron Swoboda

FIELDING AND FIELDERS

1. Match the Golden Glove winner with his fielding position.

1.	Joe Pepitone	**A.**	outfield
2.	Bobby Shantz	**B.**	first base
3.	Tom Tresh	**C.**	shortstop
4.	Norm Siebern	**D.**	second base
5.	Bobby Richardson	**E.**	pitcher

2. What amazing feat do Roy White and pitcher Harry Howell, who hurled for the team in 1903, share?

True or False.

_____ **3.** Ron Guidry was the last Yankee pitcher to lead the League in fielding.

_____ **4.** Red Rolfe, the great third baseman of the 1930s, holds the Yankee record for the highest fielding percentage at third base in one season.

_____ **5.** Moose Skowron led the League in fielding at first base at least once.

_____ **6.** Snuffy Stirnweiss' .993 fielding percentage at second base in 1948 was bested by Bobby Richardson seventeen years later.

MONUMENTS AND PLAQUES

Name the occasion of this 1949 ceremony.

Test yourself on how well you know the memorial section in the outfield of Yankee Stadium.

True or False.

_____ **1.** Whitey Ford and Mickey Mantle have adjoining plaques in centerfield.

_____ **2.** George Steinbrenner erected a plaque for himself in 1978 following the Yankees' World Championship win.

_____ **3.** Miller Huggins, Lou Gehrig and Babe Ruth are the only three Yankees commemorated by monuments in the outfield.

_____ **4.** Following Thurman Munson's death in 1979, a plaque was erected in his memory in centerfield.

_____ **5.** Managers Casey Stengel and Joe McCarthy are remembered with plaques in their honor in the memorial section.

_____ **6.** All told, there are twelve plaques in the memorial section.

7. *Bonus question.* Of the following non-Yankees, which have plaques erected in their honor in the outfield.
   a. Woody Allen   b. John F. Kennedy   c. Pope Paul VI
   d. Mick Jagger   e. Elvis Presley   f. Pope John Paul II

HOW YOU CAN BECOME A YANKEE WIFE

Those long, nail-biting waits in hotel lobbies and baseball player's hangouts must seem futile in the end, because your chances of tying the knot with the Yankee player of your dreams are about one in a million. The best advice is to plan very early. Stake out the most talented baseball player on your college, better yet on your high school, team, marry him before he becomes famous, and then pray he's drafted by the Yankees.

1. Can you match the player with the way he met his wife?

1.	Ron Davis	**A.**	She was a friend of a friend in Louisiana.
2.	Mickey Mantle	**B.**	She was a friend of a friend in West Haven, where he was a relief pitcher.
3.	Catfish Hunter	**C.**	She was a cheerleader at his North Carolina high school.
4.	Whitey Ford	**D.**	She went with him to a St. Louis high school and they lived two blocks apart.
5.	Willie Randolph	**E.**	She lived in the same apartment building and admired this articulate pitcher.
6.	Elston Howard	**F.**	She was a baton twirler for the Commerce high school rivals.
7.	Ron Guidry	**G.**	They grew up together in Brooklyn.
8.	Rudy May	**H.**	She knew him when they were growing up in Astoria, New York in the 40's.

2. His wife, Juanita, is a professional singer and has belted out the National Anthem at Yankee Stadium. He is

    a. Oscar Gamble   b. Reggie Jackson   c. Bob Watson
    d. Brian Doyle

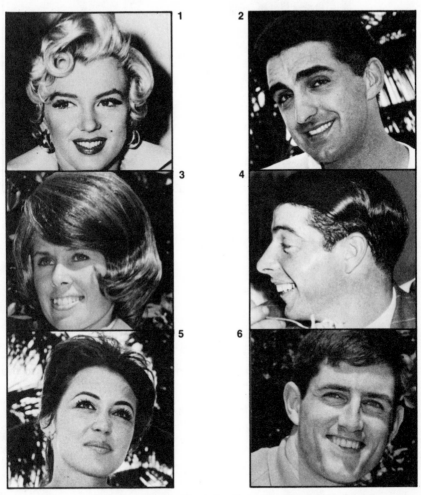

Match the Yankee wife on the left with her husband on the right.

3. How did George Steinbrenner meet his wife?

    a. at a private party at New York's "21"
    b. at a horse auction in Kentucky, prior to the Derby in 1972
    c. in the cocktail lounge of the Muehlebach Hotel in Kansas City
    d. at a dentist's office when they were given the same appointment slot

YANKEE TRADES

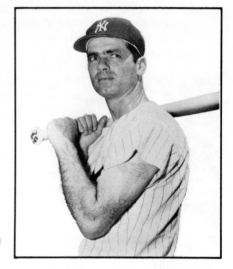

Who is this former Yankee outfielder who had a 1 – 0 pitching record during the 1968 season?

Matching questions. Match the player acquired by the Yankees in the first column with the player traded in the second column.

1. Yankee player acquired
1. Dave Righetti/Juan Beniquez
2. Brian Doyle
3. Graig Nettles
4. Ruppert Jones

Player traded in same deal
A. Jim Beattie
B. Jerry Kenney/John Ellis
C. Sandy Alomar
D. Sparky Lyle/Mike Heath

2. Match the Yankee with the team he played on before coming to the Yankees.

Player
1. Willie Randolph
2. Rick Cerone
3. Lou Piniella
4. Reggie Jackson

Prior Team
A. Baltimore
B. Toronto
C. Pittsburgh
D. Kansas City

3. Which of the following players was acquired in a trade, not as a free agent?
    a. Reggie Jackson b. Tommy John c. Oscar Gamble
    d. Rudy May

4. In the cold and windy winter of 1973 the Yankee management made a good trade involving Lindy McDaniel. Whom did they acquire?
    a. Sparky Lyle b. Graig Nettles c. Oscar Gamble
    d. Lou Piniella

1978 THE YEAR OF TURMOIL

Kicking water coolers; screaming at umpires, the opposition and fellow teammates; rejecting the press, the owner, their families; scratching and clawing their way to victory; the Yankees of 1978 were filled with memorable and barbed quotes. Can you identify the speakers in the following quotes?

1. A reserved and quiet infielder lashed out: "You get to the point where your back's against the wall, you got to come out fighting and kick some butt."

2. Many regard him as the center of the hurricane . . . "I'm not kissing anybody's backside."

3. Upon being asked to be a keynote speaker at a promotional affair, this Golden Glover remarked: "If they're looking for somebody to attend luncheons, let them hire Georgie Jessel."

4. A Pittsburgh Pirate transplant, this player astutely commented: "I was a little concerned when I first joined the club after hearing all the stories last year. I thought they wore boxing gloves instead of fielders' gloves."

5. The helmsman chose a nautical metaphor to voice his definite opinion: "A ship that sails on a calm sea gets nowhere. You've got to have a little turmoil."

6. In contrast, this seemingly pugnacious outfielder remarked: "I think this year will be very tranquil."

7. His World Series performance left many a fan and teammate gasping as well as this thirsty little utility infielder himself. "I feel like Cinderella."

8. He has an obvious taste for conflict, and after winning the playoff and World Series games this Hall-of-Famer blurted out: "This is even better than sex!"

9. In his locker room, after the smoke had cleared and the Yankees had defeated the Dodgers, this Dodger infielder sadly stated: "Blair got to me, Chambliss rolled over me, and Reggie Jackson tried to kill me."

THEY LED THE LEAGUE

(Left) Roy's surprising move to Japan for the 1980 season left many of his fans heartbroken, but it also left the #6 uniform empty for the 1980 season. Name another Yankee, a third baseman in the 1960s, who also wore #6 on his back. (Right) Who is this pitcher who led the League in strikeouts with 217 in 1964?

Can you recall the Yankee who led the American League in the following years and categories? You will find the correct answers among the players listed below.

Babe Ruth	Bobby del Greco	Frank Crosetti
Babe Dahlgren	Snuffy Stirnweiss	Ron Guidry
Reggie Jackson	Bobby Bonds	Wally Pipp
Bobby Shantz	Joe DiMaggio	Graig Nettles
Norm Siebert	Jack Chesbro	Hank Bauer
Roy White	Al Downing	Jim Bouton
Lou Gehrig	Johnny Kucks	"Suitcase" Simpson

1. As a second baseman, his .309 batting average was tops in 1945.

2. More famous as the man Lou Gehrig replaced at first base, he led the League with nine home runs in 1917.

3. He clouted thirty-two home runs in 1976.

4. Before being platooned by Billy Martin, he scored 104 runs in 1976.

5. Their separate totals of 142 RBIs earned them a tie as League leaders in 1928.

6. He won only eleven games, yet led the League with a 2.45 ERA in 1957.

7. Not only did he win forty-one games, but his 455 innings pitched was tops in 1904.

8. The last Yankee hurler to lead the League in strikeouts, this left-handed ace struck out 217 batters in 1964.

9. His 2.78 ERA in 1979, 1.04 points higher than his previous year's total, still led the League.

10. Nicknamed "The Crow," this speedy shortstop stole twenty-seven bases in 1938.

PAJAMA TALK

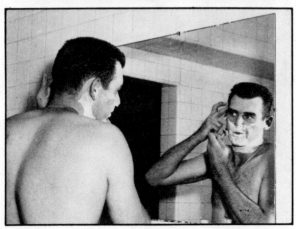

Who is this "shaving" Yankee hurler whose lifetime record is only 81 – 91, but who will always be remembered for his October miracle?

Ever wonder what the Yankees wear to bed? Here's a behind the scenes peek at what they wear—or don't wear—when they pull their shades. Fill in the blanks.

Owner ____1____ is a man not known for his modesty, but when it came to revealing what he wears to bed, he sheepishly reported that he indeed does wear pajama bottoms. The Yankees as a group, however, do not follow the example of their benefactor, for ____2____ (50%, 65%, 70%) disclosed that they sleep in the ____3____.

Famed poster star ____4____, a hero of the Boston playoff game in ____5____, intimated that pajamas are not part of his nocturnal apparel. Likewise, ____6____ disclosed that pj's are not a consideration when he retires for the evening in his posh apartment on Manhattan's fashionable upper East Side. In fact, all of the Yankee infielders and outfielders, with the exception of ____7____, the outfielder acquired from the Texas Rangers for Mickey Rivers, said that pajamas merely get in the way.

Pitchers and catchers seem to be a less hardy breed. ____8____, a premier hurler from tropical Puerto Rico, and the veteran cigar-king pitcher, ____9____, who was born on the island of ____10____, both insulate themselves from New York's harsh seasonal breezes by wearing a full set (tops and bottoms) of pajamas. Even Hall-of-Famer ____11____, the retired left-hander whose tastes and habits would suggest otherwise, reported that he wears bottoms to bed. His old battery mate, retired catcher ____12____, also wears pajamas to bed, except when he is "on the road."

Two Yankee hurlers were too shy to answer this question, but it would be unfair to report their names.

Fill in the darkened boxes of these 1965 Yankees (and one non-Yankee) as they match their wits on television's "The Match Game."

TRIVIA

Having just completed a demonstration on the art of making beer, this "captain of industry" rushed out to watch the Yankees play. Name the man and his interest in the team.

Name this hard-hitting second baseman of the 1960s.

YANKEES AND THEIR TROPHIES

Fill in the name of the Yankee player who won the following trophies and awards. You will find the correct answers among the players listed below.

Phil Rizzuto	Ron Guidry	Ralph Terry	Babe Ruth
Johnny Mize	Roy White	Mickey Mantle	Yogi Berra
Whitey Ford	Mel Stottlemyre	Billy Martin	Tony Kubek
Tommy John	Thurman Munson	Elston Howard	Lou Gehrig
Don Larsen	Sparky Lyle	Stan Bahnsen	Tom Tresh

_____ **1.** As a talented young outfielder at spring training in 1966, he won the James P. Dawson award as the most outstanding rookie. The Yankees were not to be disappointed, as he played for the team for the next fourteen seasons.

_____ **2.** Known now by younger fans as a television announcer, he won the American League Rookie of the Year award as a Yankee shortstop in 1957.

_____ **3.** As captain of the team in 1976, he won the American League MVP award.

_____ **4.** This relief pitcher won the American League's Cy Young award in 1977 for his ability to put out fires.

_____ **5.** He's now in the Hall of Fame, but as a premier catcher in the 1950s, he won the MVP award in 1951, 1954 and 1955.

_____ **6.** His sensational 2.05 ERA and 17 – 12 pitching record earned him the honor of Rookie of the Year in 1968.

_____ **7.** No baseball fan will forget his perfect game in the '56 World Series which earned him the Babe Ruth award for Series play.

_____ **8.** Though he lost (and many Yankee fans feel unjustly) the MVP award in 1978 to Boston's Jim Rice, his 25 – 3 record and 1.74 ERA still earned him the Cy Young title.

_____ **9.** In the year that Yankee Stadium opened, 1923, he appropriately won the MVP award, the only year in which he captured this title.

_____ **10.** Following elbow surgery in 1974, he won the National League's Comeback Player of the Year award in 1976 with the Dodgers.

FORD'S FOLLIES

1. In World Series competition, Ford's totals of wins and losses are tops for any major league pitcher. In eleven years of Series competition, what was his record?
   a. 17 – 11   b. 10 – 8   c. 13 – 10   d. 15 – 12

2. In a record sixteen years as a Yankee pitcher, Ford believed that the toughest hitter he ever had to face was
   a. Ted Williams   b. Al Kaline   c. Hank Aaron   d. Stan Musial

3. What superstition did Whitey have when it came to baseball?
   a. He made a point of staying out late on nights before he pitched.
   b. He would never shave before pitching.
   c. He would not eat breakfast on days when he pitched.
   d. He would lace his pitching shoes with two sets of laces in each shoe.

True or False.

_____ 4. Ford's forty-five lifetime shutouts place him at Number 1 on the Yankee shutout list.

_____ 5. In the early 1950s, Ford competed with Billy Martin for the friendship of Mickey Mantle.

_____ 6. Ford's 24 – 7 record and 2.74 ERA garnered him the Cy Young award in 1963.

_____ 7. Ford's favorite ballpark to pitch in was Tiger Stadium.

_____ 8. Ford's record of fourteen consecutive victories in 1961 is a Yankee record.

_____ 9. Russ Ford, Whitey's grandfather, was an ace hurler for the Yankees in the early part of the century, in 1910 boasting a 26 – 6 record.

_____ 10. Only Spud Chandler and Vic Raschi have higher winning percentages as Yankee pitchers than Ford (.690, lifetime).

'80 YANKEES

Identify each of the following 1980 Yankees.

YANKEE SALAD DRESSINGS

1. Match the player in the left-hand column with his favorite or preferred salad dressing on the right.

1.	Luis Tiant	**A.**	Creamy Garlic
2.	Reggie Jackson	**B.**	Oil and Vinegar
3.	Bucky Dent	**C.**	French
4.	Yogi Berra	**D.**	Thousand Island
5.	Oscar Gamble	**E.**	Roquefort

2. What's wrong with this sentence?
   A man of refined tastes, George Steinbrenner likes his salad served with Miracle Whip by Kraft.

3. Given these choices, can you guess the favorite salad dressing of the team? (Hint: It's preferred by 28% of the players.)
   a. Blue Cheese b. French c. Creamy Garlic
   d. Thousand Island

4. What is one of the reasons that Rudy May and Rick Cerone make such an effective battery combination?

TRIVIA

1. Name the only two Yankees who have won the American League Triple Crown.

2. The last triple play executed by the Yankees occurred in 1968. The three fielders involved were
   a. Tom Tresh/Joe Pepitone/Clete Boyer
   b. Bobby Cox/Dooley Womack/Joe Pepitone
   c. Bobby Cox/Horace Clarke/Joe Pepitone
   d. Dooley Womack/Bobby Cox/Mickey Mantle

3. Name the two all-time Yankee players who have played more years for the team than anyone else (eighteen).

4. Everyone should know that Tracy Stallard yielded the sixty-first home run to Roger Maris in 1961, but can you name the pitcher who gave up Babe Ruth's sixtieth home run in 1927? (*Hint:* Two years later, he was 12–0 for the Yankees.)

YANKEE SHOES

1. True or False. Yankee pitchers have bigger feet than Yankee infielders.

2. He puts out fires, hails from hell-bent Houston, Texas, and has the largest feet on the team. Name him if you can.

3. Which is the most common shoe size on the 1980 Yankee squad?
   a. 8½   b. 9½   c. 10½   d. 11   e. none of the above

4. Only one of these players has the monogrammed initials "RJ" hand-stitched into the leather of his cowboy boots. Is he
   a. Reggie Jackson   b. Roy Johnson   c. Ruppert Jones
   d. Tommy John

5. When it comes to feet, what record do Brian Doyle and Fred Stanley share?

6. While collecting his salary throwing pitches, shoe endorsements could be his real road to riches. Which Yankee hurler endorses Pony shoes?
   a. Rich Gossage   b. Ed Figueroa   c. Ron Guidry
   d. Tommy John

7. It comes as no surprise that George Steinbrenner and Reggie Jackson have big egos. But which has the bigger feet?

8. As well as can be determined, this Hall-of-Famer's shoe size of triple E is a Yankee club record. Is it
   a. Babe Ruth   b. Yogi Berra   c. Miller Huggins
   d. Mickey Mantle

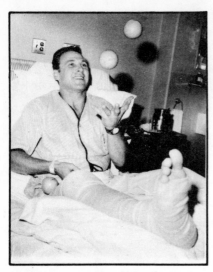

(Above) Name this juggling outfielder. (*Hint:* He never lived up to the expectation of being the next Mickey Mantle.)

(Right) Miscellaneous Yankees pose for a photographer early in the season. Can you identify this incongruous group?

1. "I've often wondered how a man who knew he was going to die could stand here and say he was the luckiest man on the face of the earth, but now I guess I know how he felt." Name the occasion and the player who spoke these words.

2. Can you put the following events from the 1960s in their correct chronological order?
   a. Bill Mazeroski's three-run homer gives the Pirates a World Series championship.
   b. Mel Stottlemyre is bought after mid-season and leads the team to a pennant.
   c. Mickey Mantle hits his long-awaited 500th home run against Baltimore's Stu Miller.
   d. Casey Stengel is fired as Yankee manager.

3. Only four Yankees were elected to the Hall of Fame in the 1960s. How many of them can you name?

4. Who won the first Mayor's Trophy Game, held at Yankee Stadium in 1963?
   a. Detroit Tigers   b. New York Mets   c. Houston Colt 45's
   d. New York Yankees

THE 1960S

They defeated the newly formed San Francisco Giants in the World Series. Name the year.

5. Yankee players won the coveted MVP award in 1960, 1961, 1962, and 1963. Can you remember the player who won it for each of these years?

6. A fabled star of the Cleveland Indians and Detroit Tigers, this slugger pounded out 374 career home runs, and closed out his illustrious career with the Yankees in 1968. Who is this baseball great?

7. Ron Klimkowski was acquired by the Yankees from Boston in 1967. In return, the Red Sox got
    a. Bill Monbouquette   b. Tom Tresh   c. Joe Pepitone
    d. Elston Howard

8. On the drizzling, chilly afternoon of September 25, 1966, Yankee fans made history while watching their team lose 4–1 to the White Sox. Why?

Identify this un-fearsome foursome of 1962.

IS THERE LIFE AFTER THE YANKEES?

You know them as the stars of today, but what will they be doing tomorrow? Can you guess the players' professional ambitions after they retire from baseball?

1. This blazing, rifle-ball pitcher, a gun enthusiast for most of his life, says that he hopes to sell guns when he retires. Name him.

2. Match the Yankee on the left with his stated ambition after baseball on the right.

   1. Eric Soderholm   **A.** broadcasting and P.R. representation
   2. Ron Davis   **B.** hypnotist
   3. Reggie Jackson   **C.** independent businessman; work with children
   4. Willie Randolph   **D.** coach at Blinn Junior College in Texas

3. Bobby Murcer says that when he retires, he hopes to
   a. be a professional broadcaster in Chicago.
   b. open up a restaurant named Murcer's in Manhattan.
   c. become an advertising executive in his father-in-law's company.
   d. make a million.

4. True or false. Rudy May intends to catch a world-record fish when he retires from the game.

5. What are the old-timers doing today? Match the Yankee on the left with his job on the right.

   1. Roger Maris   **A.** bank public relations representative
   2. Mickey Mantle   **B.** insurance executive; celebrity speaker and promoter
   3. Hank Bauer   **C.** coach and special assistant to George Steinbrenner
   4. Whitey Ford   **D.** account specialist with Reynolds Tobacco Company
   5. Joe DiMaggio   **E.** scout for the Yankees in upstate New York
   6. Elston Howard   **F.** beer distributor
   7. Johnny Kucks   **G.** liquor store owner in Kansas

THE GAMBLIN' MAN

1. Gamble is a man who enjoys the fast life. Since coming up with the Chicago Cubs in 1969, he has played with a total of _____ (4, 5, 7, 8) major league clubs.

2. If you were to travel to Montgomery, Alabama, and wanted a night out on the town, you might easily end up at
   a. a bowling alley owned by Gamble (Gamble's Spares and Strikes).
   b. a roller skating arena owned by Gamble (Oscar's Wheels and Heels Roller Derby).
   c. a restaurant owned by Gamble (Oscar's Famous Seafood House).
   d. a discotheque owned by Gamble (Oscar Gamble's Players Club).

3. Gamble was sent by the Yankees to the Chicago White Sox in April of 1977 in a deal in which they acquired infielder _____. Two years later, in August of 1979, the Yankees reacquired Gamble in a trade with Texas in which they sent the Rangers discontented outfielder _____.

4. Coming off a broken foot injury, Gamble had a spectacular half season with the Yankees in 1979 in which he batted
   a. .293 b. .324 c. .338 d. .389

5. Can you guess the two managers whom Gamble respects the most?
   a. Earl Weaver and Chuck Tanner
   b. Dick Howser and Tommy LaSorda
   c. Leo Durocher and Billy Martin
   d. Don Zimmer and Joe Torre

6. A Yankee fan would have no trouble recognizing Gamble's car, for the license plate bears the name **GAMBLE**. What kind of car does Oscar drive?
   a. Porsche b. Rolls Royce c. Mazerati d. Jaguar

FASTBALLS AND MARTINIS

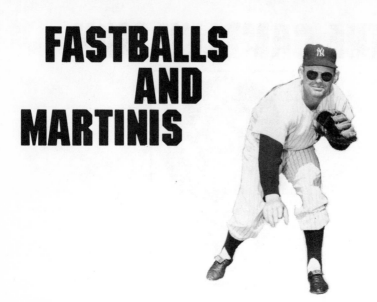

1. According to sportswriters of the day, Ryne Duren's most prominent feature was his
   a. large ears   b. lanky frame   c. Stengel-like nose
   d. bottled eyeglasses

2. As a player for the Phillies, Ryne Duren loved to make crank phone calls. He once called Grace Kelly in Monaco and told her he was
   a. President Eisenhower   b. Lord Snowdon   c. her brother
   d. Marlon Brando   e. Larry MacPhail

3. While Duren played for the Yanks from 1958 through 1961, his oldest "drinking buddy" was
   a. Mickey Mantle   b. Bobby Richardson   c. Tony Kubek
   d. Elston Howard   e. Billy Martin

4. Duren's favorite mixed drink when he was with the Yanks was a
   a. grasshopper   b. scotch and soda   c. bourbon on the rocks
   d. vodka martini

5. Duren was traded to the _____ (Angels, Athletics, White Sox, Cubs) in 1961 after allegedly causing a near riot on a Western Airlines flight.

6. In a rocky career which lasted nearly a decade how many wins did Duren achieve?
   a. 27   b. 44   c. 51   d. 82

7. Following several traumatic years in the 1960s, Ryne Duren proudly reports that
   a. he is a prospering insurance salesman in Cazenovia, Wisconsin.
   b. he coaches a college baseball team in Minnesota.
   c. he is a sports commentator outside of Chicago.
   d. he heads an alcoholic rehabilitation center in Wisconsin.

TRIVIA

Disguised in a Cleveland Indian's uniform, this player once sat in the Yankee executive offices. Who is this man?

1. Name the Yankee scout who signed up two sturdy Oklahoma boys, Mickey Mantle and Bobby Murcer.

2. Which two Yankees invested in the bowling alley business in New Jersey in the 1950s?

3. What do former Yankee players Bobby Brown, an infielder in the 1940s and 1950s, and Doc Medich have in common?

4. Most fans know that Babe Ruth hit sixty home runs in 1927, but in which year did he hit fifty-nine?

5. What do Red Rolfe, famed third baseman of the 1930s, and Jim Beattie have in common?

6. What was the name of the Yankees before they acquired the Yankee nickname?

7. The first major league game that this handsome infielder ever saw was the one that he played in for the Chicago White Sox. Name him.

8. Which player does Rich Gossage call the toughest "hitter" in the American League?
    a. Cliff Johnson   b. George Brett   c. Rod Carew
    d. Don Baylor

9. *Trivia teaser.* What was the name which former Yankee, Dock Ellis, gave to the luxury Cadillac which he drove?

ACROSS

1 Setting for the Phil Linz harmonica incident
4 Whip
8 Captain of the 1978 World Champs
14 Unpaged: Abbr.
15 Before dynamic or sol
16 Apply oil
17 Leases
19 Washes lightly
20 Where Seoul is
21 Start in
23 Bumpkin
24 Roger of the '62 World Champs
25 Intention
28 Playwright Thomas _____: (1557–1595)
29 Heathen
30 To be, in Paris
31 First-class
32 Pitcher Dock _____, owner of the "Dockmobile"
33 This infielder is called "Puff"
37 A.L. Cy Young winner, 1974
39 Sheeplike
40 Stylish
41 See 1 Down
42 Kind of energy
44 Number of homers hit in one inning by Cliff Johnson in '77
47 Tarzan actor Ron _____
48 _____ Day
49 Passing fancies
51 Ship's lowest deck
52 Catfish Hunter's wife
53 He hit three homers in the sixth game of the '77 World Series
56 Yankee outfielder who batted .314 in '78
59 Small flower
60 Blue-pencil
61 Comparative ending
62 "Mick-the-Quick"
63 Boxing ring border
64 Summer, in Nice

1978 WORLD CHAMPS

DOWN

1 1978 World Series MVP, with 41 Across
2 Unfasten
3 1977 A.L. Cy Young winner
4 Disastrous
5 "Spaceman" Bill _____
6 Bobby of hockey fame
7 Yankees' ace reliever
8 Manager of the '77 World Champs
9 Parts of a whole
10 _____ Nanette
11 Family member
12 Bobby Richardson's number
13 Nights: Abbr.
18 Jack _____, 1961–63 Yankee, whose twenty-second inning home run in 1962 won the longest game in Yankee history
22 Pitcher's stat
24 "_____ best friend"
25 Norse mythological king
26 Eye part
27 Net
29 "The Raven" poet
30 Santa's aide
31 Beer's cousin
32 And so forth: Abbr.
33 Knob
34 Knievel
35 Minute
36 Explosive
37 Charles, for short
38 Televise
40 "The Yankee _____," DiMaggio
42 ". . . _____ have another cup of coffee . . ."
43 Gold, in Madrid
44 "How do I love _____? . . ."
45 _____ Randolph, an infielder from Brooklyn
46 Egg dish
48 More arid
49 He ranks number two on the all-time Yankee base-stealing list, but his uniform number was six
50 Trap
51 Monster
53 Roofer: Abbr.
54 Yalie
55 Carey, e.g.: Abbr.
57 Wedding response
58 Small bite

125

YANKEE QUOTES

What is the most famous quip of this popular Yankee announcer?

See if you can identify the speakers of these quotes. If you can't, turn to page 71 and evaluate your Yankee addiction.

1. "Stallard wound up and delivered the 2 – 0 pitch. It was a good fast ball, but maybe he had got it too good. I was ready and I connected. . . . It was the only time that the number of the homer ever flashed into my mind as I hit it. Then I heard the tremendous roar of the crowd."

2. "Because God delays does not mean that God denies," is this active player's favorite saying from the Bible. It describes his career accurately. Name him.

3. "He would beat his own mother over the head with a bat to win," remarked American League umpire Jerry Neudecker about this pugnacious ex-Yankee. Who's the player?

4. In the tragic twilight of his career, this tearful player confessed before his grateful fans, "[I'm] the luckiest man on the face of the earth." Was this
   a. Fred Talbot b. Lou Piniella c. Luis Tiant d. Lou Gehrig

5. "Every time someone had a birthday, the guys would start yelling that so-and-so has a birthday cake. For a little fun, I'd take my clothes off and go sit on it," are words spoken by which Yankee?
   a. Brian Doyle b. Rich Gossage c. Roy White d. Sparky Lyle

ELSTON HOWARD'S TIPS ON CATCHING

Which of the following tips on catching does Elston Howard recommend and which does he not? Answer with **Y** or **N**.

_____ **1.** When I catch a ball I use my glove hand.

_____ **2.** The hardest play for a catcher is to catch the throw from right field.

_____ **3.** When I tag someone, I'm always inclined to say, "You're it."

_____ **4.** If the pitcher is throwing hard, I try to throw 'em back to him harder.

_____ **5.** Never pay attention to hitters, just yourself and your cap.

_____ **6.** Pop ups . . . forget 'em.

_____ **7.** Challenge the umpire on all his decisions. He might start seeing things your way.

_____ **8.** When the going gets tough, wear your mask up to the plate when you bat. After all, you're the only player on the team who has one.

_____ **9.** There is no better strikeout pitch than a letter-high fastball.

_____ **10.** Faster baserunners tend to steal more bases than slower ones.

(Above) What's wrong with this picture?

(Left) She watched him play for the Yankees from 1920 through 1934. No one had more to cheer about than she. Name this woman veiled in widow's weeds.

TRIVIA

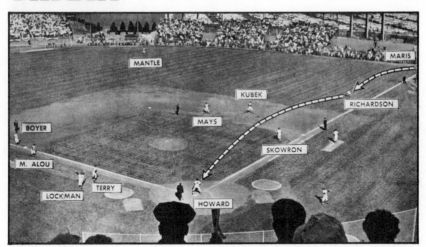

(Above) Name the year of this Series in which the Giants' Matty Alou is shown stepping on third after Willie Mays' blast to deep right.

(Right) His two weeks in the Army Reserve in October of 1963 came after a disappointing Series. Identify this utility infielder in uniform who was traded to the Phillies after the 1965 season.

THE 1980 SEASON

1. In one of 1980's most dramatic incidents, a fiery Luis Tiant hurled his mitt into a hushed grandstand, stormed off the field, and was then fined $500 because
   a. he had been unjustly accused by the umpire of throwing one of his infamous spitballs.
   b. he had refused to walk Toronto's Otto Velez in spite of direct orders from manager Dick Howser.
   c. manager Dick Howser believed that Tiant was tiring, felt that a fresh pitcher was needed, and yanked him from the game.
   d. he wanted to catch the last plane to Puerto Rico to see his family, and Howser had refused to take him out of the game.

2. Which one of the following Bombers led the team in batting with a .307 average in 1980?
   a. Aurelio Rodriguez   b. Bob Watson   c. Reggie Jackson
   d. Rick Cerone

3. Which of the following accomplishments did Reggie Jackson achieve during the 1980 season?
   a. His 41 home runs led the American League.
   b. He batted .300 or over for the first time in his major league career.
   c. He joined the ranks of Babe Ruth, Hank Aaron, Mickey Mantle, and Willie Mays by hitting his 500th home run.
   d. He sold a record number of 1.2 million pairs of Murjani jeans at his jeans outlet across from Yankee Stadium.
   e. He played in his eighth division championship in an amazing period of only ten years.
   f. "Mr. October" batted .333 and smacked two home runs in the playoffs despite the Yankee's loss.

4. This distinguished Yankee pitcher led the American League with an impressive ERA of 2.46. He is
   a. Rudy May   b. Rich Gossage   c. Tommy John
   d. Ron Guidry

5. Once again the "Great DiMag" had been upstaged. Billy Martin returned to Yankee Stadium with his peppery Oakland A's on June 21, 1980, to participate in the Old-Timer's Game. The crowd cheered Billy on so enthusiastically that DiMaggio laconically remarked:
   a. "To think he used to be my little Bobo."
   b. "What's all the fuss? Is Billy going to get the Academy Award?"
   c. "It must be his western wear!"
   d. "I always thought that George shouldn't have dumped him."

6. In compiling a phenomenal record of 103 victories and 59 losses, the Yankees marched past Boston and Baltimore to achieve their most winning season since
   a. 1927   b. 1939   c. 1961   d. 1963

1980 NEW YORK YANKEES

Bottom Row: (l-r) — YOGI BERRA, JIM HEGAN, CHARLEY LAU, DICK HOWSER, MIKE FERRARO, STAN WILLIAMS, JEFF TORBORG.
Row 2: BRIAN DOYLE, BUCKY DENT, RICK CERONE, TOM UNDERWOOD, BRAD GULDEN, BOB WATSON, RUPPERT JONES, GENE MONAHAN (TRAINER).
Row 3: GRAIG NETTLES, RON GUIDRY, FRED STANLEY, GARRY SMITH, DENNIS WERTH, DAVE RIGHETTI, TOMMY JOHN, WILLIE RANDOLPH, DON GULLETT.
Row 4: BARRY WEINBERG (TRAINER), ROY STAIGER, JIM SPENCER, OSCAR GAMBLE, BOBBY BROWN, RICH GOSSAGE, LUIS TIANT, DOM SCALA (BULLPEN CATCHER).
Row 5: BOBBY MURCER, DOUG MELVIN (BATTING PRACTICE PITCHER), JIM KAAT, MIKE GRIFFIN, ERIC SODERHOLM, RON DAVIS, RUDY MAY, LOU PINIELLA, ED FIGUEROA.

7. All Yankee news in 1980 did not emanate from the Bronx. In faraway Japan, a player named Howaito-Sun was steadily batting .290, clouting 20 home runs, and amassing 56 RBIs. Under what other name would he be better known to Yankee fans?

    a. Chris Chambliss   b. Bobby Murcer   c. Roy White
    d. Paul Blair

8. After three successive losses in the playoff championships, the Kansas City Royals were determined to undo the Yankees. Can you recall the "Yankee killer" who put the icing on the cake by blasting a *three-run* homer against Goose Gossage in the final innings of the three-game sweep?

    a. Willie Aikens   b. Willie Wilson   c. Frank White
    d. George Brett

9. It was the most controversial play of the 1980 playoffs, one which enraged George Steinbrenner. With the Yankees behind 3 – 2 in the second game, a Yankee base runner was waved home only to be nipped at the plate by KC catcher Darrell Porter. Which player was the victim of some adroit Kansas City fielding?

    a. Willie Randolph   b. Graig Nettles   c. Bobby Brown
    d. Ed Figueroa

ANSWERS

BUCKY (Page 13) **1.** c. **2.** 18. **3.** a. **4.** d and e. **5.** d. **6.** d.
7. c. **8.** c. **9.** Fenway Stadium, quite naturally.

JOLTIN' JOE DIMAGGIO (Page 14) **1.** a. **2.** 13. **3.** b. **4.** c. **5.** c.
6. a. **7.** b. **8.** False, Ted Williams led the League with a .406. **9.** d.

MARIS' ASSAULT ON THE BABE (Page 15) **1.** All were American
League pitchers who gave up homers to Maris in 1961. **2.** b. **3.** d.
4. False. **5.** False, he never did. **6.** False, he hit twenty-five at night
and thirty-six during the day. **7.** True. **8.** False, the lad was Sal Durante.
Eddie Gaedel, like Durante, made baseball history for one day by pinch-
hitting for the St. Louis Browns in 1951. He was a 3 foot 7 inch circus
midget briefly hired by Bill Veeck. **9.** Both were born in Hibbing, Minnesota.

FAVORITE YANKEE OF ALL-TIME (Page 16)
Caption Answers: (clockwise beginning at top) Bill Skowron; Steve Hamilton; Tony Kubek; Jake Gibbs; Pete Mikkelsen; Johnny Kucks.
1. Mickey Mantle. **2.** Mickey Mantle. **3.** 43%. **4.** Ron Guidry.
5. Joe DiMaggio. **6.** Reggie Jackson. **7.** Reggie Jackson. **8.** Oscar Gamble. **9.** George Steinbrenner. **10.** Billy Martin. **11.** Lou
Gehrig. **12.** Roy White. **13.** Thurman Munson. **14.** Babe Ruth.

TRADES AND PLAYS OF MIKE KEKICH AND FRITZ PETERSON (Page
18) **1.** Mike Kekich. **2.** Chris Chambliss, Dick Tidrow. **3.** Cleveland
Indians. **4.** Japan. **5.** Texas Rangers. **6.** Yankee, Cleveland, wife,
Fritz Peterson, Susan Kekich, Mike Kekich, Marilyn Peterson.

WHAT A NUMBER! (Page 19) **1.** Lou Gehrig – I. #4. **2.** Whitey Ford –
G. #16. **3.** Casey Stengel – E. #37. **4.** Bill Dickey – F. #8. **5.** Babe
Ruth – H. #3. **6.** Joe DiMaggio – A. #5. **7.** Yogi Berra – F. #8.
8. Thurman Munson – D. #15. **9.** Mickey Mantle – C. #7.

THE 1920s (Page **20**)   **1.** Lou Gehrig replaced Pipp at first base. **2.** b.
3. b-a-d-c.   **4.** Players' numbers matched the order in which they
batted in the lineup.   **5.** b.   **6.** Bob Meusel.   **7.** 21.
Caption Answers: (Page **20**) Rabbit Maranville; (Page **21**) Tony Lazzeri.

FEARSOME FOES (Page **22**)   **1.** False.   **2.** b.   **3.** d.   **4.** a.   **5.** d.
6. a.   **7.** b.   **8.** c, the Cardinals have won three World Series against the
Yankees as opposed to two for the Giants and Dodgers.

YANKEE TUBE TALK (Page **23**)   **1.** d.   **2.** "M*A*S*H."   **3.** Oscar
Gamble – B. "The Jeffersons." Bucky Dent – D. "All in the Family." Elston
Howard – C. "The Love Boat." Brian Doyle – A. "Mork and Mindy."   **4.** b.
5. Reggie Jackson.   **6.** False, he prefers Angie Dickinson.
Caption Answer: No, not to date.

KING REGGIE (Page **24**) Multiple choice: **1.** b.   **2.** b.   **3.** d.   **4.** a.
5. d.   **6.** c.   **7.** d.   **8.** c.   **9.** e.   **10.** a.
True or False: **1.** False.   **2.** False.   **3.** True.   **4.** False.   **5.** True.
6. True.   **7.** True.   **8.** True.   **9.** False.   **10.** True.
Caption Answer: (left to right) Chris Chambliss, Reggie Jackson, Teddy
Pendergrass, Paul Blair, Dom Scala.

NICKNAMES OF THE 1950s (Page **26**)   **1.** Ford – D. The Chairman of the
Board.   **2.** Crosetti – F. The Crow.   **3.** Martin – E. Schnozz.   **4.** Rey-
nolds – A. Chief.   **5.** Bauer – B. Bunky.   **6.** McDougald – G. Donald
Duck (he walked like him).   **7.** Coleman – C. Captain.   **8.** Skowron – H.
Moose.
Caption Answer: Bill "Moose" Skowron.

TRIVIA (Page **27**)   **1.** b.   **2.** Hank Bauer.   **3.** c.   **4.** d.   **5.** b.   **6.** d.
Caption Answer: 1952. Clue for experts only. The picture shows Irv Noren
playing left field for the Yankees. In 1953 Noren was only used once in the
entire Series and then as a pinch-hitter.

FIND THESE YANKEES
(Page **28**)

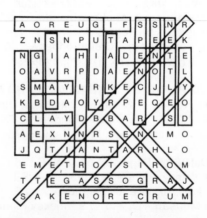

LOUISIANA LIGHTNIN' (Page **29**)   **1.** b.   **2.** d.   **3.** b.   **4.** c.   **5.** a.
6. a.   **7.** False, he finished behind Nolan Ryan.   **8.** True.   **9.** True.
10. True.

NOT FOR YOUR YANKEE PHOTO ALBUM (Page **30**)   **1.** Roy White.
2. Graig Nettles.   **3.** Sparky Lyle. (Page 31)   **4.** Jim Bouton.   **5.** Billy
Martin.   **6.** Joe Pepitone.

YANKEE SLUGGERS
(Page **32**)

```
S T R E A K ■ E R G ■ M A S S
O R A C L E ■ B O O ■ U R I S
M A N T L E ■ B A B E R U T H
E N D O ■ L I E N ■ A C T S ■
■ ■ T E N D ■ T R E ■ ■ ■ ■ ■
■ H O W A R D ■ I N R O M E
B A U E R ■ O B O E S ■ S A W
E R S T ■ B O O B S ■ A C R E
A T E ■ B Y R N E ■ O N A I R
K E L L E R ■ R I V E R S ■
■ ■ A I D ■ M O N A ■ ■ ■ ■
■ P A W N ■ B O N D ■ A R T E
D I M A G G I O ■ E L L I E S
A P I N ■ I T S ■ E V E N T S
S P E D ■ L E E ■ D I C K E Y
```

YANKEE ETIQUETTE (Page **34**)   **1.** b.   **2.** d.   **3.** c.   **4.** a.   **5.** c.
6. b.   **7.** d.

THE HOUSE THAT RUTH BUILT (Page **35**)   **1.** b.   **2.** c.   **3.** c.
4. The Polo Grounds.   **5.** The Beatles, Joe Lewis (not to be confused
with the infamous boxer Joe Louis). All the rest have performed in some
capacity.   **6.** c.   **7.** c.   **8.** c.   **9.** d.   **10.** b.

NICKNAMES (Page **36**)   **1.** DeMaestri – J. Oats.   **2.** Houk – H. Major.
3. Martin – F. Joe's Little Bobo.   **4.** Mapes – A. Tiger.   **5.** Mantle – I. The
Commerce Kid.   **6.** Munson – E. Squatty.   **7.** Lazzeri – B. Poosh 'em up.
8. Turley – D. Bullet.   **9.** Mize – C. Big Cat.   **10.** Bouton – G. Bulldog.
Caption Answer: Roy and Ray.

YANKAGRAMS (Page **37**)   **1.** Casey Stengel.   **2.** Phil Rizzuto.   **3.** Bill
Dickey.   **4.** Tony Kubek.   **5.** Fred Chicken Stanley.   **6.** Bob Turley.
7. Gene Woodling.   **8.** Whitey Ford.   **9.** Mel Stottlemyre.   **10.** Tony
Lazzeri.

TRUE OR FALSE (Page **37**)   **1.** True.   **2.** False, only the last grand slam
home run. Duke Sims hit the last.   **3.** False, he has never started in a
major league game.   **4.** False.   **5.** False, only Guidry.   **6.** True.
7. False, Tony Lazzeri.   **8.** True.   **9.** True.   **10.** False, DiMaggio won
the title.

TRIVIA (Page **38**)   **1.** c.   **2.** a.   **3.** b.   **4.** c.   **5.** Jim Beattie.
6. Mickey Mantle (1961) and Mickey Rivers (1977).   **7.** 19.
Caption Answers: (Page **38**) Sal Durante, the lad who caught his sixty-first
home run; (Page **39**) (above) Lou Gehrig; (below) Pete Mikkelsen, a
hurler from the 1960s.

ARTS AND CRAFTS (Page **40**)   **1.** Johnson – F. Shower brawling; horseback riding.   **2.** Jackson – B. Expensive cars.   **3.** Nettles – E. None.   **4.** White – G. Reading.   **5.** Lyle – J. Sitting naked on birthday cakes.   **6.** Guidry – A. Raising German Shepherds.   **7.** Chambliss – C. Collecting phonograph records.   **8.** Randolph – D. Bowling.   **9.** Gamble – H. Dancing and hunting.   **10.** Rivers – I. Gambling.   **11.** Henrich – K. Collecting cigar boxes.   **12.** c.

THE DIMAGGIOS (Page **41**)   **1.** b.   **2.** b.   **3.** b.   **4.** None.   **5.** a. **6.** b.   **7.** c.   **8.** a.   **9.** c.   **10.** b.   **11.** c.   **12.** a. *Caption Answer:* (left to right) Dom, Joe, Vince.

YANKEE LOGIC (Page **42**)   **1.** c.   **2.** a.   **3.** d (1954).   **4.** c (1903). **5.** d. *Caption Answer:* Ralph Houk. Seated on the finely manicured lawn is Mrs. Ralph Houk.

FAMOUS DATES IN YANKEE HISTORY (Page **43**)   **1.** 1956.   **2.** 1952. **3.** 1941.   **4.** 1956.   **5.** 1978.   **6.** 1923.   **7.** 1951.   **8.** 1977.   **9.** 1955.

THE 1930s (Page **44**)   **1.** d.   **2.** Mickey Mantle was born.   **3.** b-c-d-a. **4.** He replaced Lou Gehrig in the lineup at first base in 1939, ending Gehrig's streak of 2,130 consecutive games played.   **5.** d.   **6.** a.   **7.** It was off Root that Ruth hit his famous "called-shot" home run at Wrigley Field in the 1932 World Series. *Caption Answers:* (Page **44**) Lou Gehrig, Tony Lazzeri, Frank Crosetti, Red Rolfe; (Page **45**) Red Rolfe.

YANKEES AND HOLLYWOOD (Page **46**)   **1.** d.   **2.** d.   **3.** False, Guidry's favorite star is Dennis Weaver.   **4.** Gamble – B. Farrah Fawcett. Cerone – A. Al Pacino. Berra – D. Greer Garson. Tiant – C. John Wayne.   **5.** The one with Racquel Welch on the movie marquee. **6.** True.

AT THE HELM (Page **47**)   **1.** b (Minnesota Twins, Detroit Tigers, Texas Rangers, New York Yankees and Oakland Athletics).   **2.** Stengel – C. The Professor. Houk – D. Major. Huggins – B. The Mighty Mite. McCarthy – A. Marse Joe.   **3.** Bill Dickey (1946), Bucky Harris (1947–1948), Johnny Keane (1965–1966), Bill Virdon (1974–1975).   **4.** d (Huggins led the team to a pennant in 1921).   **5.** d.   **6.** All were Yankee managers.   **7.** b.   **8.** McCarthy had the highest at .614. Stengel had the lowest winning percentage as a manager at .508 (don't forget those years in which he managed such clunkers as the Brooklyn Dodgers, Boston Braves and New York Mets). Huggins was in the middle at .555.

YOGI BERRA (Page 48)   **1.** b.   **2.** a, b, c, d.   **3.** d.   **4.** b.   **5.** c.
6. 1 – 4. 2 – Boston. 3 – "Mary had a Little Lamb." 4 – harmonica. 5 – stuff. 6 – "Do it yourself." 7 – leg. 8 – hell.
Caption Answers: (Page 48) 1956; (Page 49) Ed Sullivan.

HEIGHTS AND WEIGHTS (Page 50)   **1.** b.   **2.** b-c-d-a (**B**obby Richardson, **A**ndy Carey, **B**ob Watson, **E**nos Slaughter **BABE**).   **3.** The hefty duo of Ruth and Gehrig edged out the M 'n' M Boys by some twenty-three pounds.   **4.** a – Dent, b – Dent, c – Rizzuto, d – Dent, e – Dent.   **5.** c.
Caption Answer: They were all at least six feet tall.

WIVES AND KIDS (Page 51)   **1.** a – Corna. b – Ginger. c – Eric. d – Juanita. e – Enilda. f – Nancy.   **2.** a. Ron Guidry's wife Bonnie gave birth to a boy, while Juanita Gamble was blessed with a little girl named Sheena.
3. Rizzuto – E. Cynthia. Guidry – B. Jamie. Howser – D. Jane and Jill. Murcer – A. Tori Keleighn. Randolph – C. Tanifsha. White – F. Loreena.
4. Yogi Berra, father of Dale Berra.

YANKEE HURLERS
(Page 52)

```
T E D   S O P H S   A M I R S
A G O   K R A U T   C A D E T
R O N   G U I D R Y   E L I H U
    L O N E R       M O O T
  S A O   L E F T Y G O M E Z
F I R S     S P E A R
E N S E A T   M A C E   B S H
A G E   D E B   S H E   O H O
T E N   O R E S   T R I B E S
    B R E T T     R T E S
W H I T E Y F O R D   R U N
A I D E     O U T E R
I R E N E   S A L M A G L I E
T E A S E   S P L A T   E R A
E D S E L   T A S S E   Y E T
```

BATTLIN' BILLY (Page 54)   **1.** a.   **2.** a.   **3.** c.   **4.** c.   **5.** Martin, to the delight of New York's fans, was renamed manager of the team for the 1980 season in a surprise move.   **6.** c.   **7.** d.
Caption Answer: Tex.

THE IRON HORSE (Page 56)   **1.** d. Pete Sheehy has been the Yankee trainer for over half a century.   **2.** c.   **3.** Henry Louis Gehrig.   **4.** Teresa Wright.   **5.** Babe Ruth.   **6.** One time, in 1934 with the Triple Crown.   **7.** d.   **8.** July 4, 1939. The occasion was Lou Gehrig Day at Yankee Stadium.   **9.** b.   **10.** False. The honor was denied him as he only went to bat twenty-eight times in his final season. It was ironically the first All-Star game at Yankee stadium.   **11.** d.

THE BOYER BOYS (Page 57)   **1.** Clete.   **2.** Cloyd.   **3.** Ken.   **4.** Clete.
5. Ken, by half an inch.   **6.** Cloyd.   **7.** Cloyd.   **8.** Cloyd – Alba; Clete – Cassville; Ken – Liberty.   **9.** Clete.   **10.** Ken, Clete and Cloyd.
Caption Answer: Cloyd Boyer.

NAME THAT HERO (Page **58**)   Roger Maris. He hit his sixty-first home run to break Babe Ruth's record on October 1, 1961. (Page **59**) Don Larsen. He hurled his perfect game on October 8, 1956. (Page **60**) Reggie Jackson. The scorecard shows his three home runs against the Dodgers in the final game of the World Series on October 18, 1977.

TRIVIA (Page **60**)   **1.** c.   **2.** Ralph Houk.   **3.** b.   **4.** He played for all of them.

NAME THAT HERO (continued) (Page **61**)   Chris Chambliss. The score-card records his dramatic home run which enabled the Yankees to win the pennant against Kansas City on October 14, 1976.
Caption Answers: (Page **59**) Tony Kubek; (Page **61**) b. George Stirnweiss.

ALMA MATERS (Page **62**)   Graig Nettles – San Diego State College; John Blanchard – University of Mississippi; Lou Piniella – University of Tampa; Bucky Dent and Mickey Rivers – Miami Dade County Community College; Lou Gehrig – Columbia University; Rich Gossage – Southern Colorado State College; Roy White – Compton Junior College; Jim Beattie and Red Rolfe – Dartmouth College; Reggie Jackson – Arizona State University; Tommy John – Indiana State College; Bobby Bonds – Riverside City College; Jim Mason – University of South Alabama; Bob Watson – Los Angeles Harbor Junior College; Bill Skowron – Purdue University.

CRYPTOQUOTES (Page **63**)   **1.** "Today I am the luckiest man on the face of the earth." —Lou Gehrig.   **2.** "One's a born liar, the other's convicted." —Billy Martin.   **3.** "It's great to be with a wiener." —Luis Tiant.   **4.** "Holy cow!" —Phil Rizzuto.   **5.** "I had a better year than he did." —Babe Ruth, after being asked how he felt about making more money than President Herbert Hoover.   **6.** "You could look it up." —Casey Stengel.   **7.** "I begged him not to buy that plane." —George Steinbrenner, after Thurman Munson's tragic death.   **8.** "I'm the straw that stirs the drink." —Reggie Jackson.   **9.** "From Cy Young to Syonara." —Graig Nettles, commenting on the downward turn in Sparky Lyle's career in 1978.   **10.** "It pays to save at the Bowery." —Joe DiMaggio.
Caption Answer: b.

THE SULTAN OF SWAT (Page **64**)   **1.** St. Mary's in Baltimore, Maryland. **2.** There were only Brothers.   **3.** False.   **4.** .393 in 1923.   **5.** William Bendix.   **6.** Babe Ruth.   **7.** Wrigley Field in Chicago in 1932.   **8.** 1.75 in 1916 with the Boston Red Sox.   **9.** George Herman Ruth.   **10.** Ron Guidry.
Caption Answers: (Page **65**) (above) The Babe is signing the $125,000 contract that brought him from the Red Sox in 1920. The bow-tied gentleman is owner Jacob Ruppert; (below) c.

MOST MEMORABLE GAMES (Page 66) **1.** Luis Tiant. **2.** Bucky Dent. **3.** Rich Gossage. **4.** Ron Guidry. **5.** Yogi Berra. **6.** Elston Howard. **7.** Tommy John. **8.** Reggie Jackson. **9.** Bob Watson. **10.** Catfish Hunter. **11.** Brian Doyle.

THE CATFISH HUNTER STORY (Page **67**) **1.** d. **2.** a. **3.** 5. **4.** a. **5.** d. **6.** 1. 12 – 15—B. 1969. 2. 21 – 7—C. 1972. 3. 23 – 14—A. 1975. 4. 25 – 12—D. 1974. **7.** False, Hunter was awarded the honor in 1974. **8.** c.

THE 1940s (Page **68**) **1.** b. **2.** Lavagetto broke up Floyd Bevens' no-hitter in the ninth inning of a 1947 World Series game. **3.** d. **4.** Walter Johnson. **5.** c. **6.** a-d-c-b. **7.** b. **8.** b. **9.** c. *Caption Answers:* (Page **68**) Bill Dickey; (Page **69**) (above Babe Dahlgren; (right) Frank Crosetti.

DO JOCKS READ? (Page **70**) **1.** Ron Guidry. **2.** a, d, f. **3.** All but b, Virgil Trucks. **4.** Tommy John. **5.** d.

ARE YOU A YANKEE ADDICT? TEST YOURSELF (Page **71–75**) The scoring system on page 75 will reveal the extent of your Yankee addiction.

BOMBER BOSSES (Page **76**) **1.** a. **2.** c. **3.** d. **4.** a. *Caption Answer:* (left to right) Ralph Houk, George Steinbrenner, Gabe Paul, Lee MacPhail and Michael Burke.

YANKEE ALL-STARS (Page **77**) **1.** c. **2.** They were selected for the *first* All-Star game. **3.** d. **4.** Reggie Jackson. **5.** b. **6.** Mantle was selected for sixteen years, Berra for fifteen, and DiMaggio for thirteen. DiMaggio only played for thirteen years in major league baseball. **7.** b. The National League continued its recent dominance by winning 7–5. *Caption Answer:* (left to right) Lou Gehrig, Joe Cronin, Bill Dickey, Joe DiMaggio, Charley Gehringer, Jimmy Foxx and Hank Greenberg.

MICKEY, THE MAGNIFICENT (Page **78**) **1.** b. **2.** Mickey Cochrane. **3.** b. **4.** c. **5.** a. **6.** a. **7.** Mantle – RF; DiMaggio – CF; Jensen – LF. **8.** c. **9.** b. **10.** strikeouts **True or False:** **1.** False, it's Raquel Welch. **2.** True. **3.** True. **4.** False, Mantle was in the hospital watching the game. **5.** False. **6.** False, Babe Ruth only hit 15. *Caption Answer:* (Page **79**) 1952.

SERIES TALK (Page **80**) **1.** 1956. **2.** 1962. **3.** 1932. **4.** 1941. **5.** 1960. **6.** 1952. *Caption Answer:* Rich Gossage.

STENGELESE (Page **81**)   **1.** He's a very strong person.   **2.** I'm taking a nap.   **3.** A pitcher who throws low balls.   **4.** A ballpark which lacks air-conditioning.   **5.** You can try anything against him (in this case, Sandy Koufax), but he'll still beat you.   **6.** You need twenty-five players and a manager to win.   **7.** Believe it or not, I was once young.   **8.** Haven't you ever conducted an interview before?   **9.** This is how long I'm going to have to wear my cast, reporters.   **10.** It's a fact, but look it up in a book if you don't believe me.

AS THEY WERE THEN (Page **82**)   **1.** Roger Maris.   **2.** Reggie Jackson. **3.** Mickey Mantle, with father Mutt.   **4.** Whitey Ford.   **5.** Steve Hamilton.

YANKEE HALL-OF-FAMERS
(Page **85**)

MOONLIGHTING (Page **86**)   **1.** c.   **2.** 1. Hunter – E. Fruit of the Loom, Chapstick, 2. Dent – D. Fur coats, 3. Steinbrenner – C. Miller Lite. 4. Berra – A. Jockey shorts, Yoo Hoo. 5. Jackson – B. Getty Oil, Murjani jeans.   **3.** Mickey Mantle plugging Bryllcream.   **4.** Joe DiMaggio endorsing the Bowery Savings Bank.   **5.** Luis Tiant recommending Yankee Franks.
Caption Answers: (Page **87**) (above) Enos Slaughter; (below) Hank Bauer.

YANKEE WHEELS (Page **88**) (starting in upper left and reading left to right) Jim Spencer, Bucky Dent, Whitey Ford, Rudy May (front view), Oscar Gamble, Rudy May (rear view).

THE SCOOP ON SCOOTER (Page **89**)   **1.** d.   **2.** stolen bases.   **3.** d. **4.** d. He became a Yankee broadcaster in 1957 after his retirement as an active player.   **5.** 38.   **6.** c.   **7.** d.

HOME RUN FEVER (Page **90**)   **1.** Babe Ruth (714), Mickey Mantle (536), Lou Gehrig (493), Reggie Jackson (400, as of August 11, 1980), and Rocky Colavito (374).   **2.** b.   **3.** d.   **4.** a.   **5.** Nick Etten.   **6.** Reggie Jackson, with seven at the end of the 1979 season. **7.** 15.   **8.** Lou Gehrig.   **9.** c.   **10.** John Miller.
Caption Answers: (Page **91**) (above) Mickey Mantle; (middle) Roger Maris' sixty-first home run in 1961; (below) it was Yogi's fifty-third game in World Series competition, a record for total games played.

YANKEE LOGIC (Page **92**)   **1.** d. Ruth played for both managers Huggins and McCarthy, but his feuds with Huggins were legendary, as were Jackson's with Martin.   **2.** c. Mantle and Murcer are both outfielders from Oklahoma, while Garagiola and Berra are both catchers from St. Louis.   **3.** d. Ferraro is the third-base coach under Howser. Crosetti manned the coaching box at third base for Houk.   **4.** b. Gehrig and Mantle won their respective Triple Crowns in 1934 and 1956.   **5.** a. Feller and Wilhelm have pitched no-hitters against the Yankees, while Larsen and Reynolds have pitched no-hitters for the team.   **6.** d. Stengel won the pennant in 1960 and was fired after the team lost to the Pirates in the dramatic 1960 World Series, while Berra as manager led the team to a pennant in 1964 but was quickly fired.   **7.** c. Lyle was the premier relieving ace of 1977. Murphy was the star fireman in 1939. (This **YANKEE LOGIC** section is the most difficult quiz in the book for most fans. If you managed to get all seven questions right, you can quite properly consider yourself a true Yankee trivia expert.)

TOMMY JOHN (Page **93**)   **1.** b.   **2.** d.   **3.** All have won twenty or more games in one season in both leagues.   **4.** c.   **5.** d.   **6.** 1st.

THE 1950s (Page **94**)   **1.** a.   **2.** d.   **3.** The Copacabana incident. Jones was pitted against Hank Bauer in the famous impromptu brawl.   **4.** c.   **5.** Johnny Sain.   **6.** c-b-a-d.   **7.** True.
Caption Answers: (Page **94**) Ralph Houk; (Page **95**) (above) 1953; (below, from left to right) Moose Skowron, Mickey Mantle, Yogi Berra, Hank Bauer.

HALL-OF-FAME YANKEES (Page **96**)   **1.** Red Ruffing.   **2.** Yogi Berra.   **3.** Miller Huggins.   **4.** Whitey Ford.   **5.** Lefty Gomez.   **6.** Larry Mac-Phail.   **7.** Jack Chesbro.   **8.** Earle Combs.   **9.** Wee Willie Keeler.   **10.** Lou Gehrig.

ONE LATE NIGHT AT THE COPA . . . (Page **97**)   **1.** Copacabana Club.   **2.** Yankee.   **3.** 1957.   **4.** Billy Martin.   **5.** Kansas City.   **6.** Billy Martin.   **7.** Davis.   **8.** owner.   **9.** Yogi Berra.   **10.** bouncers.   **11.** Whitey Ford.   **12.** columnist.   **13.** *Post*.   **14.** headline.   **15.** Dan Topping.   **16.** George Weiss.   **17.** Johnny Kucks.   **18.** lawyer.   **19.** lawsuit.   **20.** court.   **21.** Billy Martin.   **22.** Mickey Mantle.   **23.** Casey Stengel.

ANOTHER BRONX ZOO (Page **98**)   **1.** 37.   **2.** Catfish Hunter.   **3.** Jim Spencer.   **4.** Willie Randolph.   **5.** Ron Guidry.   **6.** Mickey Mantle.   **7.** George Steinbrenner.   **8.** Rudy May.   **9.** Jim Kaat.   **10.** Tommy John.   **11.** Reggie Jackson.
Caption Answers: (Page **99**)   False, Jim Bouton's dog's name was Rebel. False, Catfish Hunter's dog's name was Chief. False, Joe Pepitone's dog's name was Sally.

FAMOUS DATES IN YANKEE HISTORY (Page **100**) **1.** 1976. **2.** 1980. **3.** 1920. **4.** 1978. **5.** 1966. **6.** 1939. **7.** 1948. **8.** 1964. **9.** 1960. **10.** 1979.

YANKEES WHO DOUBLED AS METS (Page **101**) **1.** Yogi Berra. **2.** Marv Throneberry. **3.** d. **4.** a. **5.** b. **6.** d.

FIELDING AND FIELDERS (Page **102**) **1.** 1. Pepitone – B. First base. 2. Shantz – E. Pitcher. 3. Tom Tresh – A. Outfield. 4. Siebern – A. Outfield. 5. Richardson – D. Second base. **2.** White and Howell are the only two Yankees to have boasted a 1.000 fielding percentage for over 110 chances in one season. **3.** False, the honor belongs to Mel Stottlemyre in 1968. **4.** False, Nettles holds the record with a .975 in 1978. **5.** True. **6.** False.

MONUMENTS AND PLAQUES (Page **103**) **1.** False, only Mantle. **2.** False. **3.** True. **4.** True. **5.** True. **6.** False, only nine. There are also three monuments. **7.** c. and f.
Caption Answer: The unveiling of the outfield monuments on April 19, 1949.

HOW YOU CAN BECOME A YANKEE WIFE (Page **104**) **1.** 1. Davis – B. 2. Mantle – F. 3. Hunter – C. 4. Ford – H. 5. Randolph – G. 6. Howard – D. 7. Guidry – A. 8. May – E. **2.** a. **3.** d.
Caption Answers (Page **105**): 1 – 4, the one-time Mr. and Mrs. Joe DiMaggio; 3 – 6, the erstwhile Mr. and Mrs. Fritz Peterson; 5 – 2, Mr. and Mrs. Joe Pepitone.

YANKEE TRADES (Page **106**) **1.** 1. Righetti/Beniquez – D. Lyle/Heath. 2. Doyle – C. Alomar. 3. Nettles – B. Kenney/Ellis. 4. Jones – A. Beattie. **2.** 1. Randolph – C. Pittsburgh. 2. Cerone – B. Toronto. 3. Piniella – D. Kansas City. 4. Jackson – A. Baltimore. **3.** c. **4.** d.
Caption Answer: Rocky Colavito (Colavito did indeed pitch for the Yankees of 1968, but he is best remembered for his ability at the plate).

1978: THE YEAR OF TURMOIL (Page **107**) **1.** Willie Randolph. **2.** Reggie Jackson. **3.** Graig Nettles. **4.** Rich Gossage. **5.** George Steinbrenner. **6.** Lou Piniella. **7.** Brian Doyle. **8.** Bob Lemon. **9.** Davey Lopes.

THEY LED THE LEAGUE (Page **108**) **1.** Snuffy Stirnweiss. **2.** Wally Pipp. **3.** Graig Nettles. **4.** Roy White. **5.** Lou Gehrig and Babe Ruth. **6.** Bobby Shantz. **7.** Jack Chesbro. **8.** Al Downing. **9.** Ron Guidry. **10.** Frank Crosetti.
Caption Answers: (Left) Cletis Boyer; (right) Al Downing.

PAJAMA TALK (Page **109**) **1.** George Steinbrenner. **2.** 70%. **3.** raw, nude or buff. **4.** Bucky Dent. **5.** 1978. **6.** Reggie Jackson. **7.** Oscar Gamble. **8.** Ed Figueroa. **9.** Luis Tiant. **10.** Cuba. **11.** Whitey Ford. **12.** Elston Howard.
Caption Answer: Don Larsen.

TRIVIA (Page **110**) (top row, from left to right) Tom Tresh, Roger Maris, Joe Garagiola (the one non-Yankee); (bottom row) Whitey Ford, Mickey Mantle, and Joe Pepitone; (Page **111**) (above) Jacob Ruppert, beer czar and once a Yankee owner; (below) Horace Clarke, whose name is associated with those tarnished years of the late 1960s.

YANKEES AND THEIR TROPHIES (Page **112**) **1.** Roy White. **2.** Tony Kubek. **3.** Thurman Munson. **4.** Sparky Lyle. **5.** Yogi Berra. **6.** Stan Bahnsen. **7.** Don Larsen. **8.** Ron Guidry. **9.** Babe Ruth. **10.** Tommy John.

FORD'S FOLLIES (Page **113**) **1.** b. **2.** a. **3.** b. **4.** True. **5.** True. **6.** False, he won his only Cy Young award in 1961 when he went 25 – 4. **7.** False, Yankee Stadium. **8.** True, tied with Jack Chesbro. **9.** False, there is no relation between these ace hurlers. **10.** True, Chandler was .717 as a Yankee, while Raschi was .706.

'80 YANKEES (Page **114–115**) (from left to right, starting in upper left-hand corner) Bob Watson, Ruppert Jones, Rudy May; (second row) Tom Underwood, Oscar Gamble, Ron Guidry, Dave Righetti, Bucky Dent, Dennis Werth; (bottom row) Rick Cerone, Brian Doyle, Eric Soderholm (not pictured: Ginny Soderholm), Mike Griffin, Jim Hegan, Dick Howser.

YANKEE SALAD DRESSINGS (Page **116**) **1.** 1. Tiant – C. French. 2. Jackson – E. Roquefort. 3. Dent – A. Creamy Garlic. 4. Berra – B. Oil and Vinegar. 5. Gamble – D. Thousand Island. **2.** Steinbrenner's passion in salad dressings is Catalina, while Tommy John goes in for Miracle Whip. **3.** d. **4.** They both adore Blue Cheese dressing.

TRIVIA (Page **116**) **1.** Lou Gehrig in 1934, Mickey Mantle in 1956. **2.** d. **3.** Yogi Berra and Mickey Mantle. **4.** Tom Zachary.

YANKEE SHOES (Page **117**) **1.** True. **2.** Ron Davis. **3.** b. **4.** a. **5.** Their 7½ shoe size is the smallest on the team. **6.** d. **7.** Jackson, 11 to 9½. **8.** b.

THE 1960s (Page **118**) **1.** Mickey Mantle at Mickey Mantle Day in June of 1969. **2.** a-d-b-c. **3.** Miller Huggins, Casey Stengel, Red Ruffing, Waite Hoyt. **4.** b. The Mets triumphed by a score of 6–2. **5.** Maris – 1960 and 1961; Mantle – 1962; Elston Howard – 1963. **6.** Rocky Colavito. **7.** d. **8.** A record *low* crowd of 413 fans attended the game. The team finished last that year.

THE 1960s *Caption Answers:* (Page **118**) (above) Tom Tresh; (right, from left to right) Bob Friend, Lu Clinton, Dooley Womack, Roy White and Fritz Peterson; (Page **119**) (above) 1962; (below) Joe Pepitone, Tom Tresh, Phil Linz and Jim Bouton.

IS THERE LIFE AFTER THE YANKEES? (Page **120**)   **1.** Ron Guidry. **2.** Soderholm – B. Davis – D. Jackson – A. Randolph – C.   **3.** d. **4.** True.   **5.** Maris – F. Mantle – B. Bauer – G. Ford – E. DiMaggio – A. Howard – C. Kucks – D.

THE GAMBLIN' MAN (Page **121**)   **1.** 7.   **2.** d.   **3.** Bucky Dent, Mickey Rivers.   **4.** d.   **5.** c.   **6.** b.

FASTBALLS AND MARTINIS (Page **122**)   **1.** d.   **2.** c.   **3.** a.   **4.** d. **5.** Angels.   **6.** a.   **7.** d. (Information supplied by *The Comeback*, by Ryne Duren with Robert Drury, Lorenz Press, Dayton, Ohio. 1978.)

TRIVIA (Page **123**)   **1.** Tom Greenwade.   **2.** Phil Rizzuto and Yogi Berra.   **3.** Both are medical doctors.   **4.** 1921.   **5.** Both are Dartmouth graduates.   **6.** Highlanders.   **7.** Bucky Dent.   **8.** d. (Not Cliff Johnson!)   **9.** The Dockmobile.
Caption Answer: Al Rosen.

1978 WORLD CHAMPS
(Page **124**)

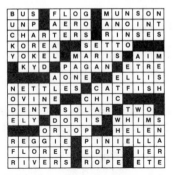

YANKEE QUOTES (Page **126**)   **1.** Roger Maris.   **2.** Tommy John. **3.** Billy Martin.   **4.** d.   **5.** d.
Caption Answer: "Holy cow!"

ELSTON HOWARD'S TIPS ON CATCHING (Page **127**)   **1.** Y.   **2.** Y. **3.** N.   **4.** N.   **5.** N.   **6.** N.   **7.** N.   **8.** N.   **9.** Y.   **10.** Y.

TRIVIA (Page **128**) (above)   The photograph shows Joe Pepitone with a glove on his left hand. In fact, Pepitone was left-handed and would have worn his glove on his right hand; (below) Mrs. Babe Ruth; (Page **129**) (above) 1962; (below) Phil Linz.

THE 1980 SEASON (Page **130**)   **1.** c.   **2.** b.   **3.** a, b, e.   **4.** a.   **5.** b. **6.** d.   **7.** c.   **8.** d.   **9.** a.